BUGLE
CALL
TO
FREEDOM

Fontanellato orphanage, later PG 49, under construction

BUGLE
CALL
TO
FREEDOM

The PoW Escape from Camp PG 49
Fontanellato 1943

Marco Minardi

Bugle Call to Freedom is a translation by John Simkins of
*L'Orizzonte del Campo: Prigionia e fuga dal campo PG 49 di
Fontanellato 1943–45* by Marco Minardi

First published in the United Kingdom in 2020 by the
Monte San Martino Trust, London

Original edition © 2015 Mattioli 1885, Fidenza
Text © 2015 Marco Minardi

This edition © 2020 Monte San Martino Trust

British Library Cataloguing-in-Publication Data
A catalogue record for this book is available from the
British Library

ISBN 978-0-9576-102-1-7

Printed and bound in the UK by Lightning Source

Contents

Acknowledgments and Translator's Note

The rights to publish *L'Orizzonte del Campo* in English were generously granted to the Monte San Martino Trust by the author, Dr. Marco Minardi, and the publisher, Mattioli 1885. Proceeds from sales of this book will go to the Monte San Martino Trust.

The English edition is a revised and updated version of the Italian edition with additional illustrations and maps.

The term *contadini*, meaning peasant farmers, which occurs frequently, has been left untranslated.

The initials PG, as in PG 49 Fontanellato, stand for *Prigione di Guerra*.

I would like to thank the following fellow members of the Monte San Martino Trust for their expertise and unstinting support in producing this edition: Julia MacKenzie, Rossella Ruggeri and Christopher Woodhead (grandson of Lt. Col. H. G. de Burgh, Senior British Officer at PG 49).

John Simkins
(son of Captain C. A. G. Simkins, a PoW at Fontanellato)

Credits

The publishers would like to thank the following for kindly allowing the use of quoted material: Tom Carver, the de Burgh family, Sue Dowie-Chambers and Jodi Weston Brake, the English family, Svetlana Hood, Tanya Kindersley, the Langrishe family, the Newby family, and Pen & Sword for Tony Davies, *When the Moon Rises* (2016), and Carol Mather, *When the Grass Stops Growing* (1997).

The publishers are also grateful to the institutions and individuals that have given permission to use the illustrations reproduced on the pages listed below:

2, 40 Centro Cardinal Ferrari, Fontanellato; 16 Ibrahim Malla; 23, 32, 51, 63, 116 from the wartime log of Lt. Mike J. D. Goldingham, a prisoner at PG 49, courtesy the Goldingham family; 28 *Home by Christmas?* Edited by Ian English, courtesy Christine and John English; 42, 59, 67 and 100 courtesy the family of Eric and Wanda Newby; 45 courtesy the de Burgh family; 76 Julia MacKenzie; 80 John Simkins; 85 Nicholas Mather; 95 Christopher Woodhead; 119 Allied Screening Commission, National Archives, Washington, DC; 122 Iside Fontana; 130 Cervi House Museum, Gattatico; 138 courtesy the family of Lt. Frank Adams.

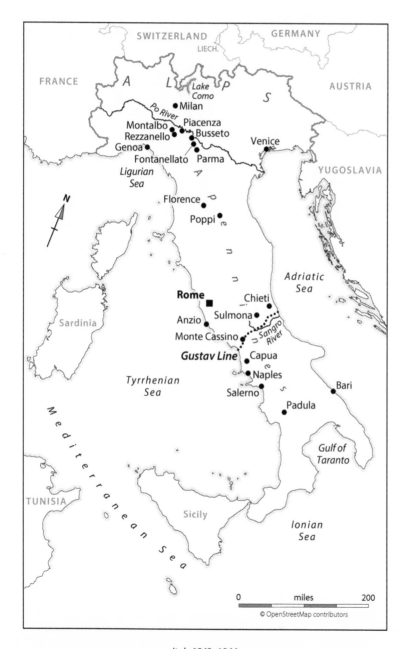

Italy 1943–1944

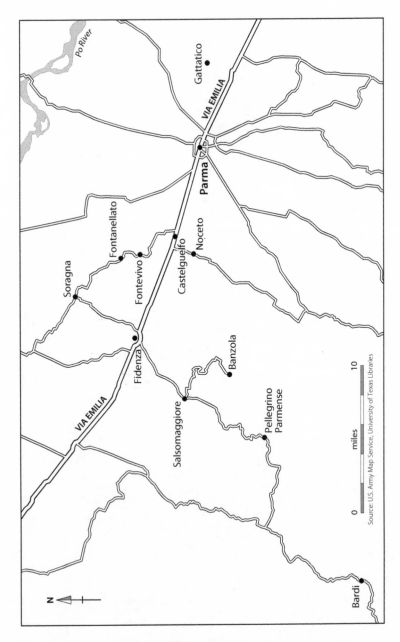

The Parma area

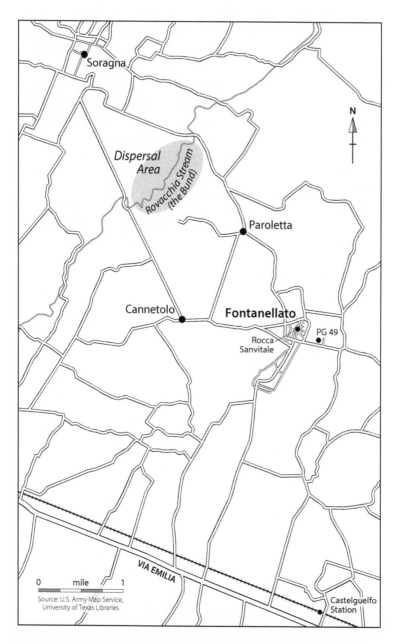

Soragna

N

Dispersal
Area

*Rovacchia Stream
(the Bund)*

Paroletta

Cannetolo   **Fontanellato**

PG 49

Rocca
Sanvitale

0   mile   1

VIA EMILIA

Castelguelfo
Station

Fontanellato and the surrounding villages

Foreword to the English Edition

To what extent are the events recounted by Marco Minardi in this book out of the ordinary?

First, let's summarise the facts. In Fontanellato, a village on the Emilian plain in the province of Parma, a prisoner of war camp had been opened on the site of a recently completed structure intended to serve as an orphanage. It was, therefore, not a barrack camp but a new building, with facilities that were more comfortable and suitable than those of the average PoW camp.

It was a "model" camp, designed to be shown off to the International Red Cross, in which about 600 mainly British officers and Other Ranks were to be imprisoned. Perhaps because it was fascist Italy's shop-window to the world, the treatment of the prisoners was particularly lenient.

The character of the commandant, Lt. Col. Eugenio Vicedomini, was also a factor. A career officer, he was at ease in negotiations and in establishing relations of mutual trust based on respect for an ethical code that bound the officers to the prisoners' British representatives.

It is possible these circumstances decisively influenced what occurred after the announcement of the Armistice. At noon on 9 September 1943, the commandant warned the British commanding officer of the imminent arrival of the Germans. The prisoners were quickly assembled and let out through a hole in the wire at the back of the camp that had been made on the order of the commandant. The camp was vacated within ten minutes and, when the Germans arrived shortly afterwards, they found no trace of the prisoners.

For the 600 ex-prisoners there began a period of uncertainty and great danger, hunted as they were by the Germans and Italian Fascists in unknown terrain. It was then that the extraordinary help proffered by the population entered the equation. At first, it was a case of spontaneous assistance from the local *contadini* (peasant farmers), who hid and fed the fugitives while German searches intensified, unavailingly. Six hundred men did not disappear into thin air; a lot of people knew where they were hidden but nobody talked.

In the following weeks the help was mainly organised by anti-fascist groups, using an extensive and well-constructed network of protection and support.

Admittedly, things did not always go smoothly. There were some leaks and the consequences were paid, above all, by the Italians who had given help. But all in all, it is astonishing how many people risked their lives to help men who had not only been their enemies but who were also, according to fascist propaganda, treacherous and inhuman.

The events prompt other considerations, too. The behaviour of civilians can only be described as "resistance", unarmed civil resistance that drew on spontaneous resources of humanity and solidarity with one's neighbour. Nevertheless, the resistance had a political character. There is no doubt that even the *contadini* in the more isolated homesteads knew of the German proclamations that threatened death to anyone who helped enemy soldiers, sheltering them or enabling their escape – and knew, too, of the cash rewards for those who turned them in. Their behaviour points to the irreversible crisis of the regime and fascist propaganda, which seem not to have had a lasting impact on Italians, much to the amazement of the British themselves.

So, was this episode exceptional? It is not easy to give an answer. Data quoted in Marco Minardi's book would suggest that, in October 1943, only 18,000 out of approximately 70,000 escaped prisoners were in German hands. But these figures relate only to the month following the Armistice. What happened subsequently? For how long did the population's assistance continue, and what form did it take? How many prisoners joined partisan groups (a choice made by few of the Fontanellato escapers)? How many were recaptured after indiscretions and betrayals?

In short, what is lacking is a wider study of relations between the PoWs and the Italian population, despite the numerous publications of memoirs and diaries to date. This is why the Monte San Martino Trust and Istituto Nazionale Ferruccio Parri hope that one of the fruits of the collaboration agreement that exists between them will be an atlas of PoW camps. Building on the list posted on the Trust's website, this would aim to bring to light what happened during escapes from camps before and after 8 September, the day it was announced that the Armistice had been signed. Only when this is done will we know if the events at Fontanellato, so well reconstructed by Minardi from British and Italian archives, should be considered out of the ordinary.

Prof. Paolo Pezzino
President, Istituto Nazionale Ferruccio Parri, Milan
(The Institute co-ordinates a national network of organisations known as the Istituti storici della Resistenza e dell'età contemporanea)

Preface

This book describes one of the best "minor" stories that go into the making of history, the official history that we study in school books. History is almost always the narration of facts and events that revolve around a few important, powerful people. Much less gets recounted about ordinary people, those who either suffer or benefit from decisions taken; about those who, when all is said and done, have really written the history. What would Napoleon have amounted to if poor soldiers had not been sent to die in the course of "his" campaigns? Or Hitler, if, in order to invade Poland, he had not sent hundreds of thousands of young men who sacrificed their lives and whose names will never appear in the history books?

History has been written, and always is written, by anonymous people in the name of, and on behalf of, some big personality.

This book demonstrates that history is also made up of minor events, which are sometimes considered insignificant in the wider historical context but are nonetheless significant. If Camp PG 49 had not existed or had been "sold out" to the Germans, or if something else had happened, this would certainly have made no difference to the outcome of the war. But a page of great humanity would have been missing, a page of uncalled-for and unexpected fellowship that today makes one proud.

The story of Camp PG 49 is unique. What happened at Fontanellato did not take place in any other prison camp in Italy.

Fontanellato, now a small town with little more than 7,000 inhabitants, lies in the heart of the Po plain: an agricultural zone noted for Parmesan cheese, fog and mosquitoes. But there is fellowship, too, rooted in the poverty that reigned in those difficult times. It is no accident that Fontanellato lies in the region of Emilia-Romagna, which in the aftermath of the war was to become the archetype of Italy's Co-operative economy. It saw the birth of numerous Co-operatives – genuine, mutual Co-operatives aimed at leaving nobody behind, possessing a spirit that, with the passing of time, has weakened somewhat – as well as economic-social development that reduced inequality.

Members of the Monte San Martino Trust at Centro Cardinal Ferrari
(formerly PG 49) in 2013, on the 70th anniversary of the escape

On 9 September 1943, following the signing of the Armistice, Commandant Vicedomini had a hole made in the camp's wire and about 600 Allied soldiers poured into the countryside searching for a place to hide and avoid capture by the Germans. The *contadini*, risking their own lives, gave help and support to these young men – hiding and feeding them and assisting them to escape. Their accounts have a bewildering simplicity ("we found them in the yard, those poor boys, what could we do?") allied with an exact knowledge of the dangers that they too were facing. It often emerges from these same accounts that the children never knew. Only a few of those who were children at the time and to whom I have been able to speak had the opportunity to see the prisoners or talk to them directly. Sometimes they did so without their parents' consent. In other cases, they learned about these events after the war.

The enormous generosity of those people wrote a shining page in a chapter of the history of the Second World War, which certainly is short of bright lights. Even today, more than 75 years later, it arouses emotion and pride among the people of Fontanellato and the inhabitants of neighbouring communities.

At times the offshoots of history extend into the present. Thanks to that courageous assistance, every year a group of young men and women benefit from bursaries that enable them to study English in the UK. The bursaries are awarded to the descendants of helper families by the Monte San Martino Trust, which was set up in 1989 by a group of former prisoners who, happily, returned home.

Within this book you will find a story of "ordinary fellowship", a story that deserves to be told in memory of all those fine people who sowed a small seed of hope in the middle of despair (and those who continue to do so). A seed of love among the horror.

Francesco Trivelloni
Mayor of Fontanellato

Introduction

By the middle of August 1943, a few weeks before Italy surrendered in the Second World War, there were 79,533 Allied servicemen held in prisoner of war camps in Italy.[*] During the progress of the war, the prisoners – who initially had been scattered throughout the Italian peninsula – had been gradually transferred to camps opened in provinces in the centre-north. On the eve of the Armistice,[1] signed on 3 September by Marshal Pietro Badoglio, the head of the Italian government, only Capua, near Naples, was still in operation among the larger camps opened in 1941 with the intention of holding the thousands of officers and Other Ranks captured in North Africa.

The steady flow of prisoners transported to the Italian mainland from the Libyan coast by sea and air had compelled the Italian military authorities to expand the camp network. Existing buildings were converted, and new construction begun in north and central Italy, in many cases alongside work camps and hospitals for the sick and wounded. But hardly ever did the camps reach the minimum standards for the treatment of prisoners set by the Geneva Conventions.

It was in the context of this gradual transformation of the prison network that Camp PG 49 in Fontanellato came into being in the spring of 1943. The village lies in the Po plain near Parma, which already contained another camp for military prisoners, PG 55 at Busseto. This was originally for Yugoslav PoWs and then Greeks, but by July 1943 it held British Other Ranks. In addition to these prisons there were

---

[*] Of these, there were 42,194 British servicemen, 26,126 Imperial (mainly from South Africa, Australia and New Zealand), 2,000 French (Gaullist), 1,310 American, 49 other European allies, 1,689 Greeks, 6,153 Yugoslavs and 12 Russians. National Archives, London, WO 224/179; Roger Absalom (1991), *A Strange Alliance: Aspects of Escape and Survival in Italy 1943–1945*. Florence: Accademia Toscana di Scienze Lettere "La Colombaria", p. 23.

two camps for civilian internees in the area, at Montechiarugolo and Scipione (Salsomaggiore).[2]

The Fontanellato building, which ended up holding hundreds of prisoners of war, had originally been intended by the church authorities to serve as an orphanage (*orfanotrofio*). It was situated at the entrance to the village next to a convent, the Sanctuary of the Blessed Virgin of the Holy Rosary, a few kilometres from the Via Emilia highway and halfway between Parma and Fidenza. Its construction, which had commenced in the 1920s thanks to donations from worshippers on pilgrimage to the *Santuario*, was completed on the eve of hostilities. At the outbreak of war the project stalled and the orphanage's inauguration was postponed until such time as the conflict should end. The military authorities selected it as a prison camp because of its structural, economic and geographic suitability.

The prisoners transferred to the new camp were predominantly British officers sourced from two camps in the lower hills of the Piacenza region – Rezzanello and Montalbo. Initially there were no more than 400 men, with the first large influx of 385 taking place on 31 March 1943. By 14 May the total had reached 540, and by the end of July it had risen to 621 – mainly junior officers (captains and lieutenants). They were for the large part British, but the contingent included a handful of Americans, Australians, New Zealanders and South Africans. There were also a number of batmen (Other Ranks) attending to the officers; these were chiefly South African and made up 129 of the July total.[3]

Daily life at the camp was not exactly arduous. Conceived as a model camp, to show off to the Swiss delegation that represented British interests in Italy, the routine was peaceful and unchanging. That, of course, did not prevent the inevitable complaints from internees. These were essentially about the lack of space available outdoors and the excessive crowding indoors. The only upsets to the routine were those provoked by the conditions of imprisonment.

This state of affairs prevailed until the announcement on 8 September 1943 of the Armistice, when the rapid turn of events also prompted the inhabitants of PG 49 to take action. All this is reported in several books published by the protagonists in the decades following the war, in papers preserved by the National Archives in London and in diaries and notes bequeathed by prisoners to the Imperial War Museum, also in London. Records held by the archive of the Italian army's General Staff in Rome are also informative, as are the memoirs of people who happened to live on the other side of the barbed wire during those months.

The first edition of this book was published in 1995. It was sponsored by the municipality of Fontanellato and the Provincial Committee of Parma to celebrate the 50th anniversary of the Italian Resistance and the Liberation. This edition,† extended and enhanced by material researched in British archives, has two objectives: the first is to revisit and update evidence of the exceptional occurrences that took place in those days in and around PG 49; the second is to stress the importance of events in the prison network in the context of the history of the Second World War in Italy. Further research is essential into individual camps and into the entire picture of Allied military imprisonment in Italy during the conflict.

---

† Marco Minardi's revised edition of *L'Orizzonte del Campo*, published in 2015 (Fidenza: Mattioli 1885).

1. The Camp

"One day, towards the end of March," recalls Wanda Newby Skof,* "the whole place became a hive of activity. Soldiers set up barbed-wire fences, electricians wired up searchlights, carpenters built barracks and sentry posts on elevated platforms. By 30 March 1943 the building was ready but empty. The following morning 650 English-speaking officers and soldiers from all over the Empire arrived. Apparently they had come by train the previous night to the nearby station of Fidenza, from various camps in southern Italy."[1]

In fact, the prisoners, who came from a number of locations across Italy, reached the new prison camp in groups between March and May. There were about 120 officers and 30 South African Other Ranks from PG 41 at Montalbo (Piacenza), followed by other contingents from the camps at Rezzanello (Piacenza), Chieti, Sulmona, Capua, Padula, Poppi (Arezzo) and others besides.[2] The new prison was intended above all to hold British officers, along with about 100 batmen, and – at least in the eyes of the Italian government – to fulfil the role of a model camp: a "wonder camp"[3] to show off to representatives of the international organisations that looked after British interests in Italy. As is evident from various memoirs of internees at PG 49, rumours had spread for some time among the camps scattered throughout the country that a new site for officers was being prepared in the north. Lt. P. J. D. Langrishe, then

---

* Wanda Skof's family, like many other Slovenes, was deported to Italy by the Fascist regime, which did not trust the loyalty of people from Slovenia, ceded after 1918. Wanda was aged ten when her family arrived in Fontanellato in 1932. After the Second World War she married Eric Newby, a prisoner at Fontanellato, whom she met while he was in hospital after the Armistice in September 1943.

imprisoned in PG 41 at Montalbo, reports: "Our Italian captors began to hint that we were soon going to be moved to a marvellous new camp where every comfort known to man would be at our disposal, subject only to the trifling inconvenience of incarceration until the Axis duly won the war but, living from day to day and distrusting all rumour, we prisoners took it all with handfuls of salt."[4]

The transfers started in March 1943. At the end of the month the orphanage already had 266 officers, together with nine NCOs and 110 ordinary soldiers. By the end of May the number had risen to 490 officers and 110 Other Ranks (the capacity was 500 officers and 120 orderlies). The first weeks of June saw the last of the transfers. The military authorities found little difficulty in adapting the existing facilities to the requirements of a new prison camp. The only problem, which appears to have delayed the transfer of the prisoners, was the existence of a large, still unconsecrated, chapel in the middle of the building on the ground floor. The army's prisoner of war department did not wish to give up this space, "both because of its size and because it constituted the central part of the building. Preventing use of it would have the consequence of dividing the building in two and making its capacity considerably smaller than expected."[5]

The difficulty was overcome by agreeing with the ecclesiastical owners to separate the apse of the chapel from the nave by use of a dividing wall. In this way it was possible "to shut off the altar and protect it both from profane use and from potential damage".[6]

The expectations of the prisoners who arrived at Fontanellato were strongly coloured by their experiences upon capture in North Africa and by the state of the camps where they had previously been held. Langrishe was in no doubt: the new camp was no other than the "promised paradise".[7] Typically, in fact, a prisoner arriving at PG 49 did so in the belief that he would find himself better off in Fontanellato than at any other camp.

A sketch of PG 49 Fontanellato by Lt. Mike Goldingham

There were, however, those who did not have any particular expectation about the new arrangements. One of these was Captain Philip Kindersley, who was among a group of about 70 officers brought from PG 66 at Capua. On the morning of 14 May they got off the train at the small station of Castelguelfo, a farming area along the Via Emilia between Fidenza and Parma, before being escorted on foot down the country roads towards Fontanellato. On the way, and well before reaching the village, Kindersley spotted in the distance "a tall modern building rising above the trees". He considered it "much too grand" for it to be suitable as a prison camp.[8] Shortly, however, he was forced to reconsider for "we perceived the familiar sight of khaki washing hanging out of the top windows. We soon reached the village. At the entrance the name Fontanellato was written boldly on a neon sign. A brand-new national orphanage rose majestically above the other houses, but the little orphans had never entered their luxurious home – they had been replaced by British prisoners of war."[9] The prisoners swung through the main gate and came to a halt "in front of the steps of our new home".[10]

The soldiers' arrival did not, of course, pass unobserved. From the start their presence aroused the curiosity of both the inhabitants of Fontanellato and the farming community around Castelguelfo station, as well as along the route taken by the new arrivals to reach the prison camp.

Bruna Chiappini, who lived at Torchio, a hamlet less than four kilometres from the railway station in the municipality of Fontevivo, spotted several groups of prisoners marching towards PG 49:

> The prisoners passed by on foot; they got off at the station and went by. All of us children – at that time I was just 14 years old – used to go onto the river bank there in order to see them. They often told us to go away, they made us get down from the embankment because they didn't want us to…I remember there were so many of them and I remember the Scots – you'll appreciate we were all eager to see these soldiers in skirts. And I remember there were so many parcels…and a strange thing, so many books, heaps of books carried on carts towards the orphanage…what on earth became of those I've no idea but I'd like to know.[11]

Wanda Newby Skof recalls that lots of people, both young and old, "were impatient to see the prisoners; most of us, including me, had never seen an Englishman".[12] However, catching sight of them wasn't that easy, even though the building looked out onto the main road.

Among the new arrivals were some who had requested to be moved to the new camp. One of these was Captain Carol Mather, who asked to be included in a contingent assigned to PG 49 with the sole aim of getting himself closer to the Swiss border – one of the targets for those wishing to regain their liberty. However, Mather had a second reason for choosing Fontanellato: he was keen to get out of PG 21 at Chieti, as it was much too big a camp and "fascist dominated". It had an unpleasant atmosphere, in his opinion, and was affected by "bad vibes".[13]

His rail journey turned out to be long and dramatic. Mather witnessed the murder of a prisoner, a RAF officer clubbed to death with rifle butts by Italian guards. The man had attempted to jump off the train as it slowed down near one of the many stations along the route. As soon as he was spotted he was surrounded by guards and finished off in full view of his companions. His corpse lay abandoned at the side of the line as the train gathered speed. For Mather and those with him it was shocking, one of many such incidents of murder and maltreatment of enemy prisoners perpetrated by guards in Italy. The Italian military, as well as the Germans during the later transport of prisoners to the Reich at the end of 1943, were both responsible.

Sometimes the convoys arrived at Castelguelfo in the dark, as happened with Mather's group. They found themselves stranded in that "ghostly" place in the rain, their morale at its lowest ebb and without transport to take them to Fontanellato. At one blow the high expectations fed by the departure from Chieti gave way to disappointment.[14]

Major Richard Carver, the stepson of General Bernard Montgomery, enjoyed a different reception at Castelguelfo on 30 May, as he recounts: "We…were met by the Camp Commandante [Lt. Col. Eugenio Vicedomini] and the interpreter [Captain Jack Camino, the second-in-command] who knew England well and had acquired some English habits."[15] Carver adds: "We marched the four miles to the camp along a hot and dusty road through flat, rich countryside, but received rather a shock when we got there. We had expected a small senior officers camp but this place housed 500 officers with 100 soldiers to do the cooking, etc."[16]

As they marched from Castelguelfo to Fontanellato the prisoners wondered what awaited them and tried to imagine the new camp – without much success. Langrishe recalls the rumours that spread through the column of marching men after their journey from Montalbo. "One voice said the camp was in huts, another that it was another castle, till finally we came in sight of a huge new brick-built edifice. It was so impressive and modern that nobody considered for a moment that this was our destination till the head of the column turned into the gateway."[17]

Once through the gates the new arrivals were made to wait in the large space below the steps leading up to the building. The Montalbo group had to wait there for more than an hour before being allowed to enter. Ill-feeling spread rapidly among the officers. Impatient at the treatment, many of them protested by sitting on the ground while the flag was hoisted, provoking inevitable reprimands from Commandant Vicedomini and the guards.[18] As Langrishe recalls, this unforeseen event resulted in the search of the new arrivals being postponed until the following day, to the prisoners' great relief. Thankful to the commandant for not having spun out the entry procedure still further, the officers were at last able to enter along with their possessions, "including the cat which had been brought from Montalbo on a lead, to the amazement of the Italians".[19]

In general, the men were pleased with the new camp, although there were some complaints. This was to be expected, considering the segregation and loss of freedom. "After the filth of Padula it was a joy to be in a place like this," says Lt. Ian Bell.[20] It wasn't long before PG 49 was christened "the Ritz of prison camps". The building's massive size reassured the prisoners. Lt. Dan Billany describes it as dominated by "a vast pompous façade in what might be called the Municipal-Flamboyant manner".[21] In the memory of others, it was "our own Buckingham Palace".[22]

After passing through the gates and climbing the steps, one came across a spacious living area that was the centre of the four-floor building and which served as the heart of the prisoners' communal life. On two sides of this hall were bedrooms, dormitories and services. In the basement there were bathrooms, showers, a pantry and three canteens furnished with large tables set with white tablecloths and good-quality cutlery and glasses.[23]

The representative of the Swiss Legation was left with an excellent impression after visiting the camp on 14 May 1943. After all, the building had been selected and made ready for precisely this reason: to represent a model camp for officers that could be shown to international authorities without losing face.

Captain Leonardo Trippi, the man in charge of the Swiss Legation, described PG 49 in his final report as "the best among those we have visited here. The lodgings and the interior arrangements – facilitated by the capacious building – are comfortable and the camp is well organised. The morale of the internees is high and they are on excellent terms with the Commandant."† The high standard of the facilities particularly impressed the head of the legation – and that could not have been otherwise. Thanks to an "up-to-date plumbing system"[24] on each floor, there were "two toilet-rooms with washbasins provided with 16 taps (mirrors are on the walls), five closed-in Turkish water closets and three flushed urinals". The officers' bathroom contained 12 showers and the Other Ranks had a separate bathroom with six showers (hot water available on Tuesdays).[25]

Other areas were set aside for stores, a library, reading rooms, workshops and dining rooms for officers and their batmen. The camp also had a surgery in the charge of an Italian medical officer. Under his orders were three medical officers and an attendant chosen by the prisoners. For those who had come from camps at Bari, Sulmona and Montalbo, PG 49 "was heaven".[26]

"It was reputed to be the best camp in Italy," says Bell. "It was a great relief to find that we no longer had to scrounge around the camp for fuel for our *stuffas* [stoves]. All

---

† See Appendix 1.

that messy and laborious work in cooking our food under trying conditions was now over."[27]

Thanks to an excellent cook in the person of Lt. Leon Blanchaert, a Belgian serving with the British army, the prisoners were able to eat at table on dishes consisting of the contents of Red Cross parcels and the food provided by the Italian authorities. At Fontanellato, prisoners were at last able to sleep on beds instead of on wooden bunks.[28] They had lockers, regularly ate fruit and vegetables and were allowed to purchase a daily ration of *vino*.[29]

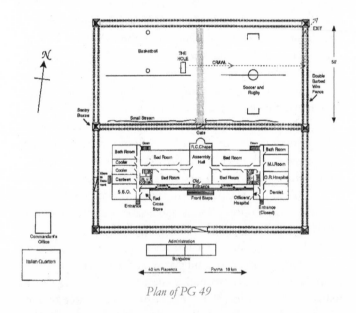

Plan of PG 49

Indeed, for alcohol, the prisoners were permitted an aperitif (vermouth) at lunch and a glass of "vino *molto ordinario*"[30] at dinner. To be on the safe side, the Senior British Officer took control of the distribution of alcoholic drinks. He requested, and obtained, permission for an officer of his choice to handle this. Thus took shape "Tommy's Bar", situated in the hall and run by Tommy Pitman, a RAF pilot. When presented with a chit – each prisoner was given a certain number of these – he would hand over an alcoholic drink. The chits served as the camp's currency, which soon came to be used to buy goods contained in Red Cross parcels.

In effect the huge hall became the fulcrum of the camp's social life. It was the scene of cultural and recreational activity, above all games of cards. But there was also scope for performances, language courses, presentations and lectures. On one side there was a small chapel for Catholic officers, while two other rooms were reserved for non-Catholic services; in fact, the camp had two chaplains, one Presbyterian and the other Anglican.

Although the building met with general approval, there was no lack of criticism of its soundness. Lt. Eric Newby recalls that "it was a large, three-storeyed building with a sham classical façade, so unstable that if anyone jumped up and down on one of the upper floors, or even got out of bed heavily, it appeared to wobble like a jelly. To those of us who were lodged on one of these upper floors, it seemed so unstable that we were convinced that if any bombs fell in the immediate neighbourhood it would collapse."[31]

A good deal more concrete were the complaints about restrictions on the space at the prisoners' disposal, the lack of privacy and the excessively bureaucratic rigidity that regulated the camp. The summer heat played a part in subduing the protests, even though the space available outdoors was very limited.[32] The only outdoors area comprised a courtyard about 18 by 90 metres at the back of the main building, enclosed within a double barbed-wire fence. It was "paved with large pebbles similar to those on the beaches back home", says Bell.[33] In April a second plot was made available. This was intended to be an exercise field, for football, rugby and basketball. On the day it was opened "we all rushed into the field like a lot of youngsters".[34]

Enthusiasts among the prisoners were given the task of levelling the ground and getting rid of the rocks and holes that ruled out sport of any sort. At the prisoners' request the camp commandant decided to entrust them with the job of smoothing out the ground. After the Senior Officer had given the go-ahead, the men of PG 49, armed with hoes and shovels, immediately set to work to level the exercise field – and, at the same time, prepare an escape route.

Indeed, the Senior Officer had authorised an escape plan hatched by a group of the detainees. Taking advantage of the work in progress, this involved digging a ditch in which two or three people could lie down. Hidden by planks of wood lifted from the prisoners' beds, and by earth from the field, they would wait for dark and then escape. That part of the camp was not illuminated at night and, emerging from their hiding place, they would presumably be able to crawl undetected as far as the double fence. Pulling this up, they would manage to get out and away without leaving a trace. When hidden in the hole, the "buried alive", as the nominated escapers came to be known, would breathe fresh air through specially adapted tubes.

The escape day dawned. Two officers were chosen to be the first to make the attempt. As night fell, with the searchlights trained on the building, the escapers got through the fence and vanished into the dark – free. From that point on, the versions about what actually happened are not consistent. There is disagreement about the total number of escapes as well as about how they were kept secret from the guards so they could be repeated. Among the various accounts given in diaries and books, those of Langrishe and Captain Ian English seem to be the most detailed but, at the same time, have the greatest discrepancies between them.

According to Langrishe, the scheme worked successfully for ten consecutive days, enabling about 20 prisoners to flee. In his account it was the Senior British Officer himself who called a halt to the escape plan, decreeing it ended and allowing the guards to discover it. In English's account, however, there were no more than two escapes and only five officers got away. The biggest challenge was how to hide the fact, on the morning after an escape, that men had slipped out during the night. This was necessary if more prisoners were to get out the following night.

Before every roll-call the procedure was for the Italian officer to be handed a list of the sick and the rooms where they were in bed. After the roll-call, which took between 20 minutes and an hour, the officer inspected the sick. Langrishe says the plan was for prisoners to feign illness and, when the inspection was over, for them to move from their sick bed to that of the escaper. This was done by using the two flights of stairs at either end of the building. The inspecting officer would go upstairs and confirm that the prisoner absent at roll-call was in fact in a sick bed. After the inspection, on reaching the end of the corridor he would go to the floor above, using the stairs on the opposite side to the ones he had just climbed.

It seems that this zig-zag route allowed the accomplices who had feigned sickness, surrounded by other prisoners returning from roll-call, to slip quickly out of their beds, reach the corridor and shoot up the stairs on the opposite side of the ones being used by the guards. In this way they could get into the beds of the fugitives before the arrival of the Italian officer. And so on, day after day, with more and more accomplices involved and fewer and fewer prisoners present at roll-call. Langrishe writes: "The cover plan was maintained for about a week after the last pair had left and then, one fine summer morning, the deception was lifted. The Italians simply could not believe their eyes, twenty short of total strength!"[35]

According to English's report, there were only two escapers the first night and three on the second.[36] He says the deception plan involved the use of dummy heads placed in the escapers' beds in order to deceive the inspection officer. Although his account would appear the more convincing, in both versions escapes concluded with the capture and return to Fontanellato of the fugitives.

Once the escape had been discovered it took the guards some days to reconstruct the plan and find the ditch used by

The Italian guards discover the ditch in the playing field used by five escapers on 7 and 9 May, as pictured by Lt. Mike Goldingham

the escapers – renamed "the Wooden Horse of Fontanellato" by the men of PG 49.[37] Commandant Vicedomini decided to illustrate his report of what had happened with pictures of the escape plan. To the prisoners' amusement, a number of photos were taken and drawings made. Langrishe recalls several internees looking out of the orphanage's windows and witnessing various stages of the escape being immortalised on paper and film. This prompted much laughter among the officers. He says: "An Italian soldier was sent to sit in the hole and several exposures made from different angles, to the accompaniment of loud jeers and cheers from the windows of the orphanage."[38]

Among the originators of the plan was Captain Tony Roncoroni, a second row forward in the English rugby team and the British Lions at the beginning of the 1930s. He was very popular within the camp. With two others (Captain Dominick Graham and Captain Peter Joscelyne), he absconded for only a short time, barely a day, but just enough to taste a bit of freedom before being forced back behind the walls of PG 49. However, the first two fugitives (Lt. Jimmy Day and Captain Michael Ross) were close to attaining their objective when they were caught in the Como area near the Swiss frontier.

With the digression of this first escape attempt concluded, work resumed on the exercise field. It was completed by the Italian guards. The area was reopened on 24 May, with additional restrictions to those originally intended: access was limited to two hours in the morning and two in the afternoon, and to a maximum of 100 prisoners at any one time.

Of course, these curbs provoked complaints from the detainees, who were forced to stay shut in the building for much of the day. Lt. Col. D. S. Norman, the prisoners' representative at the time, delivered a formal complaint to the camp's authorities and informed the Swiss Legation. The prisoners' dissatisfaction came to the notice of the War Office in London, which advised putting off any dramatic form of protest, at least for the time being. The aim was to safeguard the good relations that were being established between the detainees and the camp's commandant, not without effort. A formal complaint might have brought about the replacement of the commandant and made diplomatic efforts up to that point a waste of time.

Football was the most popular activity among the prisoners who used the exercise field. Organised tournaments were keenly followed by those who did not take part and by the guards. Excitement among the followers helped keep prisoners' morale high. This was already buoyed by reports on the war's progress, which was going better and better for the Allies. Right through the summer, says Langrishe, "rugby football and soccer were played furiously throughout the tropic heat of the day, to the amused interest of our guards who regarded this as proof, if proof were needed, of the proverbial madness of the English".[39]

A mere few hundred square metres of ground were insufficient to meet the needs of the 600-plus men shut up in the camp. Many of them were forced to endure a sedentary life that raised tension and caused the young officers to get on each other's nerves. In an attempt to make up in some way for the lack of exercise, the commandant introduced weekly walks. Soon they took place two or three times a week. In groups of up to about 140 at a time the prisoners were allowed to march along the surrounding country lanes "under a general parole, which covered the period when we were actually outside the gates", says Newby.[40] The detainees, who were "heavily guarded", always kept their promise, at least during the march. As soon as they were back, however, the young officers considered themselves at liberty to go on plotting to escape.

Leaving at 7 a.m. and returning before it got hot, they still found a way to make life difficult for their escorts. Typical of this was when a group of prisoners caused alarm among the Italian soldiers accompanying them. Rather than an attempt to escape, it was more of a challenge – a demonstration of their superiority over their jailers. Shortly after leaving, the leaders of the column accelerated, keeping up a brisk pace (140 steps to the minute, rather than the usual 120). This put their escorting guards under severe pressure and, finding themselves at the rear of the column, they tried to stop the march. The vanguard, however, had no intention of obliging and the prisoners pressed on at a great rate until they reached the camp. As punishment, the prisoners engaged in this helter-skelter were made to walk slowly, "at a funereal pace".[41]

In his account, Langrishe suggests this was not a unique occasion. "For these [walks] we donned our smartest kit and always kept a spanking pace along the local country roads where our route took us and it was not unusual for a walk to return to camp with only the Italian Orderly Officer and the *Carabiniere* sergeant, the military escort having fallen by the roadside being unable to keep up with us."[42]

The weekly outings meant a lot to Lt. Tony Davies:

Once a week those who elected to, were allowed, under heavy guard and on parole, to go for a walk.

The prisoners would turn out as immaculately dressed as possible, boots shining and uniforms neatly pressed; and, marching in columns of threes, were led by Prevedini for a good two hours' ramble round the countryside. I looked forward to these excursions with great impatience. Apart from our natural enjoyment of the exercise and fresh air, we soon acquired a pretty exact knowledge of the lie of the land for some miles round the camp – a knowledge put to very good use later on.[43]

Even though instinct was against doing such a thing, the prisoners did entertain thoughts of escape during the excursions. Newby, like many others, relished those marches through the countryside of the Po plain:

> We marched at a tremendous rate, glad of the exercise and taking sadistic pleasure in exhausting our guards who were mostly small men with short legs. We marched along flat, dusty roads; past wheat fields; fields in which forests of Indian corn were growing and into which I longed to take flight; along the foot of high green embankments which protected the land from the torrents which at certain seasons poured down from the Apennines into the River Po; past huge fields of tomato plants and sugar beet, groves of poplars, endless rows of vines and great rambling farmhouses with farmyards full of cows and pigs and ducks and geese, and red-roofed barns with open doors in which we could just see great mouth-watering Parmesan cheeses ripening in the semi-darkness. Where we went we saw very few people. Perhaps they were told to keep out of the way when we went past.

Looking at this burgeoning countryside in the spring and summer of 1943 it was difficult for the most optimistic of us to believe that Italy was in danger of collapsing through lack of food, although it was obvious that the Italian army was very badly fed. One had only to look at the exiguous rations which the soldiers who guarded us drew from their cookhouse. And here, so far as I could make out, there were no organisations as there were in Britain to make their life more supportable. No volunteer ladies dishing out fish and chips to them, and great squelchy, jam sandwiches, and cups of orange-coloured tea, and, saying "Hello" and asking where they came from, making them feel that they were doing something worthwhile which somebody cared about. They were like souls in limbo or a lot of untouchables in Hindu India, lost in the low-lying ground which no one ever visited, somewhere between the railway workshops and the cantonment.[44]

Among the many restrictions imposed on PG 49's detainees, the ban on contact with the local population was the hardest to enforce. This was due to the converted building's shape and position.

Appearing at the windows could be extremely dangerous, as Kindersley relates. Shortly after his arrival, while he was enjoying the unmissable glass of vermouth at "Tommy's Bar", word got around that two officers who had recently absconded were about to return to the camp. "Natural curiosity prompted me to look out of the window, and I was so absorbed in the proceedings that I failed to notice an Italian officer who was shouting and waving his arms in my direction. I was brought to my senses by the sharp report of a pistol, and two bullets embedded themselves in the wall below the window. In an instant, the few people in the bar were on the floor, and a small procession was led out of the door by John de Bendern on his hands and knees."[45] Newby recalls that close supervision of this intensity was relaxed only after 25 July 1943, the day Benito Mussolini was deposed.[46]

Billany discovered on arrival that:

> the sentries here are much quicker on the trigger than at Rezzanello. If you look out of the window after dusk, they do not waste time writing out a report about it. They shoot. And after lights out, if they see or hear anything they don't like, they shoot again – at random, anywhere into the building. It would have seemed strange in England to go to bed and sleep calmly while men outside were firing rifles in at the building, but you very soon got used to it. So far nobody has been hit, though there are holes in the bedroom walls. It sounds much more alarming than it is.[47]

The bullet holes in the hall's internal walls sparked Newby's imagination. Some of the shots "used to come whistling through the windows – the glass had been blown out long ago – and bury themselves in the walls and ceiling of the bar, which had the same ecclesiastical décor as the chapel below. These bullet holes gave the place a raffish appearance, like a middle-western saloon built by some renegade, gun-toting priest."[48]

For some time, anyway, this manner of surveillance did not change, despite the prisoners' many protests. At the root of these dangerous and potentially lethal measures lay the Italian guards' extreme difficulty in curbing the prisoners' exuberance and their desire to communicate with the outside world. Rifle shots, however, did not have much success in frightening the detainees, who continued appearing at the windows and challenging the armed guards – especially when girls from the village passed by.

On warm evenings the young females found the walk even more attractive. It was "one of the few places where they could flirt", Tom Carver was told by his father, Richard.[49]

> Showing off their brown legs beneath cotton farm dresses, they would stroll slowly past the camp fence, as if on a catwalk, arm in arm either with each other or with their mothers or grandmothers. The guards in the watchtowers would turn their backs on the camp to talk to them while behind them the occupants of "Tommy's Bar" looked on from a distance.
>
> It wasn't usually long before one of the prisoners, fired up by the *vino lavorato*, would yell a crude invitation. The NCO in charge of the guards, under pressure to defend his womenfolk from slander, would scream at his men who would turn around and loose off several rounds in the direction of the windows. This would provoke more taunts and insults from the prisoners and in turn more shots. Sometimes a prisoner who felt a bullet singe his ear would go too far and yell something about the NCO's mother, and then an order would be yelled in the guardroom below followed by the crash of boots up the marble stairs. Tommy would be told to close up the bar and the Italians would retreat, grumbling about how the British couldn't handle their drink.[50]

For anyone coming from the town, once past the fence the promenade proceeded to the left, along the road leading to the cemetery. This flanked the right-hand side of the building, which also had a large number of windows. Many years after the end of the war, Wanda Newby Skof wrote:

We couldn't often see them [the prisoners] from the main road which passed in front of the building because they were forbidden to look out of the windows. If they did look out the sentries had orders to fire on them, which they did from time to time although no one was ever injured. The only reliable way to see them was to pass in front of the building and turn left into the road to the cemetery: from that side some of them could be seen craning out of the windows and waving.

It is the custom all over Italy to visit the cemetery and take flowers to the graves, usually on Sundays or on the anniversary of a death. Once the prisoners had arrived, the dead found themselves in perpetual company. Never could they have been visited by so many young girls. [51]

It was in just these circumstances that Newby first set eyes on the girl who would become his wife after the war had ended. Wanda was to recall: "I had seen him once before when he had waved to me from an upper window and I had waved back." [52]

Despite everything, time seemed to stand still at PG 49. Confined to the huge central living area and the sports field, the prisoners occupied themselves by playing cards, lounging on camp beds, drawing, painting, reading, studying Italian or German, following history lessons, staging a play, taking exercise – anything to keep up their spirits. For them, as officers of the British Empire's army, it was not easy to be deprived of command after months of training and warfare. The sudden loss of status – and to be in prison no less – weighed heavily on their state of mind. [53] The long, uneventful and never-ending day seemed like a form of torture. "Life in prison was like an interminable Saturday afternoon…The war was still raging all around but they were no longer a part of it – it was hard not to feel a failure in some way and the gung-ho language of the camp often masked depression."[54]

At night it was not unusual to hear officers talking in their sleep, crying out or shouting orders, reliving moments of battles in North Africa, or dreaming of battles taking place without them. During the day, if not participating in the various activities, officers simply sunbathed at the bottom of the sports field. Some competed in interminable rugby sevens tournaments, dominated by the South Africans, or in six-a-side football matches.[55] Others played basketball on a court at the north end of the fenced area of PG 49. A brook ran across the site available to the prisoners – home to four goslings that the guards had brought from a lake nearby.[56]

Fontanellato orphanage under construction shortly before the outbreak of war.
The cemetery is at the top right

There were other activities besides those of a sporting or intellectual flavour. To avoid the ever-present risk of sinking into unhealthy apathy, some of the detainees set up as businessmen. Richard Carver came across "Opportunities Ltd.", run by F/Lt. Bill Rainford, a RAF pilot, which claimed to offer "every service except escape". Another business was

"Rack and Ruin", run by an engineer from the Midlands, which offered a mending and repair service.[57]

Official records say little about personal relationships, but the memoirs are less reticent. Stories of friendship, dislike and close affection emerge from both diaries and autobiographies. Friendship is vital when it comes to sharing escape plans and it became essential after the camp was evacuated in September 1943. Within the prison's walls at least one love story apparently unfolded, as is related in the semi-autobiographical work *The Cage*, by Billany and Lt. David Dowie. Without ever spelling out "the love that dare not speak its name",[58] the two officers talk of their existence in that cage (the camp) under the constant gaze of hundreds of eyes and in the complete absence of privacy.[59] They stayed together after the mass escape on 9 September but never reached home. They were last spotted in the Apennines, 70 miles from the Front Lines. The circumstances in which they died are unclear.

Three years later Billany's family received a parcel containing the manuscript of a book. It was accompanied by a note from the person in whose hands the two fugitives had placed the manuscript; they had requested that it be forwarded should they not return to claim it at the end of the war.[60]

To help the prisoners face up to life behind barbed wire, many of them lent on experience acquired during their school years. In particular, as Tom Carver writes of his father, "to anyone who'd grown up in an all-male boarding school the routines and the tribalism of PG 49 were very familiar".[61]

As Major Carver noted, among the numerous groups and cliques was one that stood out: a small band of well-born officers who came from a very different background from the rest of the prisoners.[62] They appeared to consider the war a game demanded by others, one in which they were invited to take part as guests; their only obligation for the moment was to sit things out until they could inherit their aristocratic titles.[63] They were always clustered together, as if they were a herd apart, expressing themselves in an argot largely incomprehensible to others, communicated by references, events and hints that only members of their social class would have been able to fathom. As an artillery officer, without an aristocratic title and landed property, even Lt. Col. H. G. de Burgh, when he became Senior British Officer, was excluded from this circle.

Eric Newby, right, with two other prisoners

Tom Carver, drawing on his father's diary, tells how the prisoners who belonged to White's Club in London would regularly meet in the hall after dinner to play baccarat. They used to play for large stakes, honouring their debts by instructing their banks in St. James's. During the day they would organise prisoners' races. Each "owner" would train his own team, monitor the athletes' diet and health and get them fit. The "owners" could be seen timing their athletes as they sprinted round the sports field just as if they were at Newmarket with their beloved thoroughbreds.[64] One day during a race, says Tom Carver, Newby miscalculated the number of laps and slowed down, thinking he had reached the finishing line. At the end of the race a disappointed member of White's Club came up and asked him if by any chance he had thrown it. The problem was that Newby had had no idea how much his trainer had bet on him to win.[65]

It was not only the elite clique who placed bets. Other prisoners used to wager on sports events staged between opposing factions. Despite the heat of the Po valley summer, matches and tournaments became more and more frequent behind the wire. Bets were placed on football, rugby and basketball – even on "boat racing", which seemed to be just as popular among the officers.

Firms of bookmakers sprang up to regulate and take in the bets.[66] The rules of the boat races were simple: small boats made of cork competed along a ditch fed by a spring near the sports field. The ditch was 4.5 metres long, with a steady flow of water. At one point it ran underground in a drainpipe, causing moments of great tension until the boats emerged to reach the finishing line near the barbed-wire fence. The water, meanwhile, went on its way before losing itself in the surrounding fields. Kindersley was captivated by this activity. "I at once came to the conclusion that all the officers taking part in this sport were completely round the bend. However, within a fortnight I was one of the most enthusiastic of boat owners!"[67]

At Fontanellato, as elsewhere in the PG network in Italy, there was a constant shortage of food. This contravened Article 11 of the Geneva Convention spelling out the duty of the imprisoning authority to ensure that the quantity and quality of food were adequate. To make up for the Italian state's shortcomings, the tinned food and luxuries that came from the Allies in the form of Red Cross parcels were soon assigned to feed and nourish the thousands of men interned in Italian prisoner of war camps. At Fontanellato, Commandant Vicedomini oversaw the distribution of this food scrupulously and guaranteed that every prisoner should receive one parcel a week. In many cases elsewhere, however, the authorities ended up using the precious contents of these parcels to punish and blackmail prisoners – that is, when they didn't actually profit from the parcels themselves.

Food and tea, above all, were often exchanged between prisoners and guards and, through the latter, between prisoners and the townspeople. Each parcel might contain tins of biscuits, jam, meat, margarine, carrots or tomatoes; sometimes there was bacon, cheese, fish paste, sugar, tea, chocolate, condensed milk and soap. There might also be raisins, porridge oats, sweets, tinned pudding or pancake mixture. The men of PG 49 greatly appreciated all this produce, and so too did the guards and inhabitants of Fontanellato. In some weeks the exchange between the prisoners and their minders was frenetic: cigarettes for good-quality vermouth seems to have been the most common swap. "There were some good parties and some rather awful ones too," says Newby.[68]

The nuns of the convent of the *Santuario* situated next to the orphanage had been charged with handling the camp's laundry. A strange rapport developed between them and the British soldiers, comprising presents and messages of support. Newby recalls how "from time to time we discovered little notes wrapped up in our clean sheets or tucked inside our shirts, which said that those who had washed them were praying for us".[69] In turn, the prisoners used to pass messages of gratitude to the nuns, and sometimes small gifts. Chocolate, and so on, from the parcels was hidden among the dirty linen.

The Senior British Officer and the Italian commandant remained on good terms throughout the six months in which PG 49 operated. Three British officers had spells as camp leader: initially Lt. Col. D. S. Norman, known among the prisoners as "no nonsense Norman"[70]; replaced in May by Lt. Col. N. E. Tyndale-Biscoe, "Tyndale Biscuit", who was well liked by the young officers. He had arrived with a contingent of colonels and majors, including Lt. Col. Hugh Mainwaring, from a senior officers' camp at Poppi in the

Tuscan province of Arezzo but he was not in charge for long. Mainwaring himself gave frequent, highly popular, lectures on military strategy, drawing on experience gained on the staff of General Montgomery. Those best received were the talks "covering the period from El Alamein to the advance into Tunisia".[71]

Tyndale-Biscoe's successor was Lt. Col. H. G. de Burgh, probably the most influential of the trio and a leading actor in the dramatic mass escape on 9 September 1943.‡ Strict but reasonable, de Burgh demanded discipline and dignity from everybody.

Lt. Col. H. G. de Burgh

---

‡ Lt. Col. Hugo de Burgh, R.A., was captured at Fuka in North Africa at the end of June 1942. Before arriving at Fontanellato on 8 August 1943 he had been in PG 75 at Bari, PG 38 at Poppi and PG 202 (Lucca hospital). Reports by his fellow prisoners at the end of the war give only praise for how he conducted his role at Fontanellato, his management of relations with Commandant Vicedomini and his organisation of the escape. National Archives, London, WO 208/4247, extract from report PW/REP/Italy/208 by Major G. D. H. Flowerdew.

Newby writes: "Under him the *orfanotrofio* began to resemble the prison camp in Renoir's *Grande Illusion*."[72] Upon his arrival he "was so horrified by the lackadaisical, demilitarised state in which he found us all, that he immediately organised the camp on the lines of an infantry battalion, in companies with company commanders".[73]

In contrast, there was just one Italian commandant during the whole of PG 49's existence, in the person of Vicedomini. Previously he had been in charge of the prison at Gonars (Udine) intended for Yugoslav troops. This later became a camp for interned Slovenian and Croatian civilians deported from territory invaded by the Italian army of occupation.[74]

He had a staff of six officers, including his second-in-command, Captain Mario Jack Camino, who had the job of interpreter, as well as about 60 soldiers comprising *Carabinieri* and members of the *Alpini* regiment. Camino was originally from the Aosta valley; apparently he had an English mother and was married to a British citizen. It seems he had been compelled to return to his home country shortly before the war, after 25 years spent in Britain, in order to avoid internment, the fate that befell Italians as citizens of an enemy country.[75]

Among the other officers under Vicedomini's command was Lt. Orazi, who had worked for an Italian company in Chicago. It seems that he, too, was on good terms with the prisoners and that he often hung back to chat to them. Another of the officers was Lt. Paolo Prevedini, who before the war had worked for a long time for a well-known English travel agency, acting as a guide for British tourists in Italy. When he spoke English, according to Davies, one could detect a trace of Cockney.

It is evident from comments in the prisoners' diaries and autobiographies that Vicedomini was liked and trusted by the majority of the English officers. He was a veteran of the First World War who "had fought with the British and was almost openly Anglophile".[76] For this reason, and because the prisoners respected his methods, he was considered an excellent soldier. Captain Robert (R. N. D.) Williams describes him as "an affable and efficient person",[77] while Newby says he was "a regular *colonello* of the *ancien régime* who found himself in sympathy with our colonel, who came from the same sort of background as he did".[78] He was "conceded to be 'all right', a 'good chap'".[79]

Williams says Vicedomini "believed that the right way to treat us was like school children – give us enough to do and we would keep out of mischief; so we were allowed much in the way of art requisites and materials for our plays and concerts".[80]

It was a style of command, marked by human compassion,[81] that allowed him to carry out his duties as a soldier faithful to his oath without having to compromise his own moral probity. A style that seemed to reassure a good number of the internees, who viewed him as representative of the class of career officers with monarchical leanings which opposed the alliance with Hitler and thus the war against Britain. Prisoners thought he was a true gentleman, writes Adrian Gilbert in his book *POW: Allied Prisoners in Europe 1939–1945*. At "Tommy's Bar" the word was that he had been an international bridge player[82] – a fact that naturally increased his popularity among the young officers.

Kindersley describes Vicedomini as "a very pleasant person who did everything to make our lives as bright as possible".[83] In the opinion of Davies, he "gave the impression of being an excellent soldier. He was no fool and had the situation well under control; there were no loopholes. Unlike so many of his brethren, he realised that it was a PoW's duty to try and escape, just as it was his duty to try and stop us. Because of his efficiency and foresight, he kept the advantage firmly with himself."[84]

There are several reports of an incident involving Lt. Jack Comyn, who was discovered attempting to slip out of the camp disguised as a worker. He was taken to the office of Commandant Vicedomini, who looked him up and down in that way he had. "*Tenente* Comyn, my sentries on the wire might have shot you. And then what would your mother have said?"[85]

But not everybody appreciated his paternalistic methods in dealing with situations, which could become tiresome and irritating. The truth, Tom Carver points out, is that the officers were angry, above all, for having been captured. A sense of profound shame hung over their imprisonment, stoking intolerance and anger that were directed mainly at the guards. The latter often reacted clumsily to the humiliating treatment they received at the hands of some of the internees. Unlike Vicedomini, the guards did not earn the prisoners' respect. Newby says: "For…the wretched soldiery who guarded us, the privates and the NCOs, with their miserable uniforms, ersatz boots, unmilitary behaviour and stupid bugle calls, we felt nothing but derision."[86]

An assortment of prejudices, beliefs and a feeling of superiority fed the often-sarcastic comments, and these were not related only to the guards' military rank. One episode narrated by Williams explains the attitude to the Italian guards better than others. It took place at the changing of the guard. "Part of the Guard Mounting ceremony called for a 'fix bayonets' and, as they fixed, they all shouted 'Savoia!' One day a number of us watching from upstairs windows shouted 'Oi!' in unison with their 'Savoia!' There was a moment's silence, then the Guard Sergeant yelled '*Disgrazia!*' [*Disgraziati!*] and before long the building was full of angry little *Itis*[§] trying to discover the culprits, but by then we had all dispersed and they never succeeded."[87]

Newby was to confess, several years later: "How arrogant we were. Most of us were in the *orfanotrofio* because we were military failures who had chosen not to hold out to the last round and the last man."[88] Probably in order to blot out "the uneasy feeling that we should not be alive, the sense of failure",[89] the officers resorted to hatching escape plans.

---

§ Disrespectful term for Italians.

Besides, it was a soldier's duty to try to escape. Each plan was scrutinised by an escape committee or the Senior Officer, who would decide if it were worth persevering with. Newby says: "There were a lot of attempts at escape, some successful, some of them funny."[90] For example, Claude Weaver, an American pilot with the RAF, refers to an attempt to escape that he and Sgt. W. Wendt, a fellow American, made through the camp sewer. "We got some distance down the pipe, but then found that the contents had caked and blocked the exit, so we had to come back."[91]

Captain G. F. Spooner, for his part, says he "worked on two tunnel schemes but after a time I gave these up in favour of a private scheme of my own. The plan was to attach myself to a party going for a walk after the guards had made a count of the numbers. This plan was finally postponed because of rumours of an imminent Allied invasion."[92]

On a clear day the detainees could make out the mountains on the horizon, beyond which they would be free. Langrishe writes:

> There were days of great beauty to be fully appreciated by those upon whose hands time hung; there was the mighty chain of the Alps running in a half-circle from the west to the north-east, a chain of snow-clad giants, sparkling in the clear morning sunshine. There was the mighty massif of Mont Blanc, poised in mid-air on a cushion of misty blue above the plain; further to the north could be seen the great shoulders of Monte Rosa beyond which lay Switzerland, a land of freedom, and all its shimmering brethren in their ice-clad majesty.[93]

For many, the scenery meant much more than a beautiful view; it was an explicit summons to grasp freedom at the appropriate moment.

After the first, dramatic, escape plan using Fontanellato's "Wooden Horse"[94] had been put to bed, other schemes were conceived during following months; this despite the fact that the building's structure – it was a single entity, on several floors and near the village – did not lend itself to escapes. It meant that excavating tunnels – the usual method of escaping – was extremely hard work. Despite this drawback, there were prisoners prepared to spend a large part of their time digging tunnels.

Dominick Graham, a captain with the Royal Artillery, says the basement was the only place from which a tunnel could be dug, and that the three possible sites in it were searched regularly. "By the end of August, after the tunnel had reached five feet below the basement level, work had to be stopped owing to flooding. Water level defeated all the tunnels at Fontanellato."[95]

A report of an ambitious and technically complicated scheme comes courtesy of Newby, who took part, at least at the planning stage:

> The head of the shaft of this tunnel was in a bedroom on the *piano nobile* [main floor] of the building, practically in mid-air, and the shaft went down through the middle of one of the solid brick piers which supported it and down into the cellars. When we reached mother earth, somewhere below the floor of the cellar, if ever, he [the proposer] had planned to construct a chamber, in which the spoil could be put into sacks and hauled to the surface...The shaft had a false lid, designed and made by a South African mining engineer. It was a marvellous piece of work – a great block of cement with tiles set in it that was so thick that when the *Carabinieri* tapped the floor of the bedroom with hammers, which they sometimes did, the lid gave off the same

sound as the rest of it. This lid was so heavy that special tools had had to be devised to lift it.

Newby says the work was abandoned because events rendered it unnecessary.[96]

A similar project had a very different outcome. This also involved excavation of a tunnel, but one leading from the orphanage's lower flight of stairs. On this occasion the tunnel was successfully completed, if not without difficulty. But when the moment came to put the escape plan into operation de Burgh called a halt to it. "Events in Italy clearly pointed to a possible Armistice," says Kindersley.[97] He adds that "this was a wise decision, as the last thing we wanted was to lose our pro-British commandant".[98]

Lt. Mike Goldingham's sketch of the news flash about Mussolini's fall, 25 July 1943

At the end of the summer, recalls Davies, "the morale of the camp was exceptionally high. Every day the Italian radio and newspapers spoke of fresh reverses and disasters."[99] The prisoners followed the Italian military collapse with great attention and growing excitement. "The Axis were cleared out of Africa and the invasion of Sicily was well under way," says Davies. "Even the most ardent pessimist felt that Italy's days in the war were numbered, and that an invasion of the mainland would bring about the collapse of the Fascist regime."[100] Rising tension in the camp was palpable. Davies again: "If and when the Italians dropped out, there was a strong possibility that we might all be transported to Germany. We knew, moreover, that it would be done quickly and efficiently, with no warning at all."[101] Langrishe records, "Our guards began quite openly to talk of going home and seeing our families again."[102]

Events came to a head on the evening of 25 July. Larry Allen, an American war correspondent, had the job of listening to the daily broadcasts on the clandestine radio assembled by the prisoners. He would tune-in to the BBC and circulate a summary. The briefing posted on that day was more concise than usual, and to the point. "Flash. Benito finito!"[103]

"Suddenly, sensation!" says Langrishe. "The afternoon of 25 July was electric, radios outside the camp blared and without any warning a small crowd came streaming down from the village shouting and dancing in the street – 'Mussolini has fallen, Mussolini has fallen'. The pathetic Italian soldier guards, C3 to a man, poured out of their huts tearing portraits of Il Duce from the walls and jumping on them with their boots…Mussolini had fallen and, strangely, the millions of Italians who recently appeared to worship the ground on which he walked now reviled him and cursed him to perdition as the man who had ruined his country – which in truth he had done by electing to tie it to Hitler's coat tails."[104]

The confusing and contradictory events of those days were accompanied by outbreaks of jubilation that left the officers of PG 49 dumbfounded. The explosion of joy among the population and the camp's military was inexplicable in the light of what was taking place. Italy was sliding towards a traumatic military defeat, the forerunner of new disasters from which it was advisable to steer clear as much as possible.

As the euphoria of the evening of 25 July dissipated, everything seemed, deceptively, to return to normal. The authoritative *Corriere della Sera* newspaper filled its pages with praise for the exploits of the British Eighth Army. This was, notes Langrishe, "clearly a step in preparing the Italian people for a change of side in the war. When it actually arrived on Italian soil, the people could rely on the British army to regard them as friends again." This was all the more extraordinary because "only shortly before, the papers had been reviling 'the barbarous Anglo-Saxon' fliers who had been dropping bombs on their sacred soil".[105]

But, more pragmatically, what really interested the prisoners was to know, in Langrishe's words, "how would the German army react? After all, we were sitting in our camp in the Po valley some 500 miles at least away from the then front line. Not only that, but we had seen German infantry marching about on our road past the camp and [heard] rumours of a whole division encamped in the neighbourhood for training. We would not have long to wait."[106]

2. The Escape

On 25 July, the news of Benito Mussolini's fall spread rapidly through the camp. Apparently one of the *Carabinieri* was the first with the news, but that is not certain; anyway, it spread quickly from room to room. "Everybody here is very excited...but nobody knew quite what it meant," writes Lt. Dan Billany.[1] "The atmosphere had that hush, that sense of waiting which one associates with declarations of war. We did not have to wait for the formal announcement. Something immense had happened."[2] Then the camp's loudspeakers confirmed the removal of Mussolini and the appointment of Marshal Badoglio as the new head of government. "Uncontrollable grins came up on to our faces," says Billany.[3] But he adds: "We drew no facile conclusions. A year of prison has taught us elementary patience."[4]

In the days that followed, in the words of Captain Philip Kindersley, "behind the wire nothing ever changes".[5] The prisoners did, however, have some indication, what with the correspondence arriving sooner, for example, and censorship becoming much less strict. The guards, too, appeared to abandon the hateful practice of shooting at the prisoners if they approached the building's windows in order to attract the attention of passers-by.

On the outside, among the townspeople, signs that change was afoot were much more obvious. On the day after 25 July, Lt. P. J. D. Langrishe was among those selected for the routine walk outside the camp. It wasn't hard to notice "an extraordinary visual change...We suddenly realised that virtually every representation of the hated emblem, the fasces – the bundle of rods – had been blotted out...and such slogans as 'Long live the King' appeared."[6]

Days of waiting ensued. But these were also days of hope, nourishing the men's desire to get back home or at least rejoin their regiments. The downing of an Allied aircraft in the sky above the camp served to bring home to everyone the reality of war and imprisonment. The story is told by Kindersley:

> Some ten days before the Armistice, a formation of seventy-five Flying Fortresses flew over the camp. We noticed that one of the planes was in difficulties; smoke was pouring from its engines and it was gradually losing height. Then a white speck appeared in the sky – one of the crew had baled out. The parachutist made a leisurely descent and it looked at one moment as if he would land conveniently in the prisoners' playground! He did not reach the camp but came down in a field about two miles away.
>
> There was great excitement among the Italian soldiery. A light tank of very antique vintage roared off down the village street, followed by a platoon of Italian infantry, armed to the teeth and travelling in a truck. A tank and a platoon of Italian infantry stood quite a good chance against an unarmed, and probably injured, American airman. Meanwhile, the plane came lower and lower, and shortly after passing over the building banked steeply and disappeared behind some trees. A column of black smoke rose into the sky – the plane had crashed, killing the remainder of the crew. The truck and tank returned victorious. The Italian soldiers proudly displayed the parachute and then lifted the injured American airman from the back of the truck. After examination by the Italian doctor, it was discovered that the American had broken his toe. The Italian army had gained a glorious victory at last.[7]

The same episode – differing a little in the facts – is related by Tom Carver, relying mainly on the diaries of his father, Richard, the stepson of General Montgomery, and Lt. Col. Tony MacDonnell ("the Gloomy Dean"), who was to be Richard's fellow fugitive.[8]

The fighting continued even though political events seemed to suggest it would soon conclude. The Allied aircraft flying over Italy were by now capable of striking anywhere.[9] Lt. Stuart Hood was to admit later that he had not really understood what was going on.

> We knew very little. Ever since – in July – an Italian soldier had walked into the camp office, taken Mussolini's picture from the wall and smashed it under foot, we had lived in a kind of limbo, blown about by rumour, wild hope and despondency [...]
>
> We presumed that the Allies would land in the north and nip the peninsula in two. We imagined that the Germans would be moving in, reinforcing, taking over. We did not know whether or not they would be interested in the fate of four hundred officers.
>
> There were other imponderables: what would the Italian commandant do? Would his men obey him? What were people like outside the wire? How would we react to freedom? How far had captivity unmanned us?[10]

Nobody attempted to escape at this time. MI9, the British Secret Service department concerned with prisoners in enemy hands, had succeeded in communicating to camp leaders the order to stay put.

The department's chief, Brigadier Norman Crockett, who had worked for the London Stock Exchange before the war, was anxious about the possible outcome of an escape *en masse* from Italy's camps.[11] He feared the consequences, following Italy's defeat, of thousands of Allied servicemen loose in the countryside, risking everything while attempting to reach safety or rejoin their regiments. On the one hand, they might get in the way of Allied troops advancing north; on the other, they might become a target and an object of revenge for those Italians still faithful to Mussolini. All this sprang from the belief that General Montgomery would rapidly advance up the Italian peninsula and, in a few days, reach the Po valley. As it turned out, this belief was mistaken.

Since 7 June, most of the camp leaders had received the "stay put" order in case the British and American forces should disembark on the mainland. They were told explicitly to keep an eye on their men and to prevent them from fleeing while awaiting the arrival of the Allied forces.[12] Lt. Col. Hugo de Burgh, the Senior British Officer from 8 August, was aware of the order that had been transmitted by the BBC and received by the clandestine radio built by PG 49's prisoners shortly after the camp had opened. Knowing that the majority of the camps possessed radios, MI9 had provided camp leaders with a code enabling them to interpret BBC broadcasts. The British government sent senior officers silk handkerchiefs, imprinted with the HK code ciphers, hidden within the PoWs' care parcels.

An important factor was the co-operation of the Revd. Ronald Selby Wright, who was well liked by the British troops and who had until recently broadcast an extremely popular weekly programme called "The Radio Padre", intended for forces on the Front Line. At the beginning of summer 1943 the military chaplain had secured a transfer, as had long been his wish, and the transmissions ended. Recalled in haste and in a rage, he was persuaded to resume the broadcasts, in which messages were inserted using the HK code.

As time passed, suspicion grew that the "stay put" order was an error. Concern intensified after the Armistice was announced and it became increasingly doubtful that the Allied troops would be on the scene before the Germans arrived. Moreover, by then few had faith that Article 3 of the Armistice would be respected.

This stated: "All prisoners or internees of the United Nations to be immediately turned over to the Allied Commander in Chief and none of these may now or at any time be evacuated to Germany."[13]

At Fontanellato, the day of 8 September, when it dawned, was not like all the others. Although the war was being waged, everything had been got ready for the festival of Santa Maria Immacolata. In the fields behind the camp and next to the convent the event had, as usual, attracted hundreds of people from the surrounding area. Lt. Ian Bell says: "The weather was extremely hot, and it seemed that the world and his wife were out of doors."[14] The presence of hundreds of bicycles parked in front of the camp gave a clue as to the size of the crowd, and a large proportion of the Italian soldiers based at the camp took advantage of a brief spell of leave to wander about with their girlfriends and family members.

That year, however, the festival could boast a very special attraction – the British prisoners – and the orphanage became the obligatory destination for those there on the day. A never-ending stream of men, women and children filed past the camp, intent on seeing the prisoners. "It was difficult to say which was the bigger attraction – the fair or ourselves!" Bell reports. "Only here and there did we receive a wave from a sympathetic soul."[15]

As was usual in the evening, a large number of prisoners were crammed inside the hall, many of them absorbed in games of bridge. Others were finalising the scenery of a stage play that was due to open. The rest were on their beds or perched on the sills of the many windows that looked out on the road. It seems that these men were the first to realise that something had happened, when the hitherto carefree atmosphere among the crowd gave way to panic. Bell recalls: "Those who lived outside the village were frantically striving to reach their bicycles. Others were blocking the road by gathering into small groups."[16]

Meanwhile, two prisoners confined to the sick bay learned the news directly from the radio blaring from the Italian guard huts. "At about a quarter to seven," writes Lt. Eric Newby, "while Michael [Gilbert] and I were lying on our beds sweating…a programme of music was interrupted and someone began reading a message in a gloomy, subdued voice. It was to the effect that the Italian government, recognising the impossibility of continuing the unequal struggle against overwhelming superior enemy forces…had requested an armistice…Badoglio's announcement provoked some mild cheers from various parts of the building and a more extravagant display of joy by the Italian guards outside our window, which we watched a little sourly."[17]

Wanda Skof (later Newby), right, and friends on bicycles near Fontanellato

The guards given leave of absence hurtled back to the camp. Their shouts and behaviour brought home to the internees what had really happened. "Peace!", "Armistice!", were the words heard most often. Excitement spread within the hall too, but, passing among the bridge tables, Bell heard the bid "three spades" coming from someone who in no way was going to allow anyone to interfere in his final game of bridge.

Kindersley describes the scene: "At eight in the evening of 8 September, the bar had its usual crowd of clients. Spirits were high. Suddenly, there was a great commotion outside. Boys and girls were tearing down the street on bicycles shouting *'Pace! Pace!'* An Italian sergeant was standing on his head in the courtyard – strange behaviour even for an Italian sergeant – and others were dancing and embracing each other."[18] Kindersley continues:

> Immediately he heard the news, Colonel de Burgh held a conference with the Italian commandant, and then ordered all the officers and ORs to assemble in the main hall. The noise was worse than the parrot house in a zoo. There was little room to move and precious little air to breathe. Colonel de Burgh mounted the rostrum and there was an immediate hush. I shall never forget the tense atmosphere as we waited to hear what the SBO had to say. One could have heard a pin drop. Colonel de Burgh never wasted words and he made no exception on this occasion.
>
> "Gentlemen," he said, "I have been informed by the Italian commandant that the Italian government has asked for an Armistice. Beyond that I know nothing, but the commandant has promised to keep me in immediate touch with the situation. In the meantime, it is absolutely essential that everyone keeps perfectly calm and behaves like a British officer. No one is to look out of the windows or make demonstrations of any kind with the civilians. No one is allowed outside the building. Everyone will parade in the courtyard at nine tomorrow morning, when I will give you further details of the situation."[19]

From the start of his spell as Senior British Officer, de Burgh had imposed tight discipline, thinking ahead and preparing his men for just such a situation as the signing of the Armistice had brought about. The officers had been organised into four companies, with Other Ranks forming a separate one. There was also a small HQ company headed by de Burgh himself. Discipline was essential if they were to take advantage of the favourable circumstances now presenting themselves.

What was particularly promising from the internees' point of view were the good relations that their commander had established with Lt. Col. Eugenio Vicedomini, the camp's commandant. As de Burgh testified after he had been repatriated on 5 September 1945, he had been informed by Vicedomini of a notification that the Italian authorities had received from the German command. This was that, contrary to what had been settled by the Armistice, all Allied prisoners on Italian soil would be transferred to Germany. Asked by de Burgh to be informed about an imminent transfer, Vicedomini reassured him of this and also promised to keep an eye out: a squad of soldiers on bicycles would constantly patrol the surrounding area and warn of the approach of German contingents. At any rate, de Burgh acted in the knowledge that he was drafting an escape plan with the complicity of the camp commandant and possibly of the Italian guards.

On 8 September and the following day the two officers met frequently to discuss the details and timing of an escape. It was indeed on 8 September that the risk of being taken away by the Germans became a reality. Many of the prisoners were mentally prepared to flee, even though the order was to "keep calm". Few managed to sleep that night, thinking of what might happen the next day. Many hoped that the Allies were close to disembarking in the Gulf of Genoa, from where they would quickly reach the Po plain and release them.

There was a strong possibility that the Italian soldiers might discard their uniforms and desert the camp during the night. Accordingly, de Burgh instructed Major Carver to stay awake and, if necessary, order his platoon of engineers to substitute for the Italians at the main gate. Meanwhile, other prisoners would take the places of the *Alpini* and the *Carabinieri* along the perimeter. "We must not allow a breakdown in order."[20] Nobody should take the initiative and organise escapes. All this, however, proved unnecessary. The guards stayed at their posts that night and would have continued to do so until their own commander ordered them to demobilise.

The following morning the situation seemed to deteriorate from one moment to the next. Vicedomini invited de Burgh to despatch one of his officers, accompanied by an Italian officer, outside the camp to investigate an initial hiding place in case of a rapid evacuation.[21]

Lt. Col. Hugh Mainwaring, who had been put in charge of emergency situations (a German attack or the danger of deportation to Germany), was given the job of carrying out this inspection. He surveyed a number of places around the camp that had already been singled out during the weekly walks conducted that summer.

Mainwaring gave his own account in his escape report:

> Nothing occurred till 0730 hrs, 9 Sep, when the Italian commandant again came in. He said that the situation had deteriorated and asked that I should be allowed to go alone on a reconnaissance to find an area in which the P/W could be hidden. He gave me a map and indicated the direction he considered the best. I left the camp at 0800 hrs and found a most suitable place along the banks of a small river, where there was very thick undergrowth. This was about six miles from the

camp. I returned at 1200 hrs and within ten minutes the alarm was sounded.[22]

Tension was palpable in the camp that morning. The order was still "keep calm" amid reports of clashes between Italian and German detachments at Parma and Piacenza. Vicedomini was aware that the Germans would soon reach Fontanellato and occupy both the camp and the village. He and his men would mount a defence if that occurred.[23] Kindersley says that de Burgh was at first prepared to offer his own men for the defence. He then retracted the offer, thinking this would embarrass the British government. He opted for an eventual evacuation, should it prove possible, and transfer of the men to the place already identified by Mainwaring. Meanwhile, the prisoners were told to go back to their rooms and await further orders.[24] Each man got ready whatever he needed for the following 48 hours; the rest was in the rucksacks that they would recover after the Germans had left the camp.

Lt. Mike Goldingham's drawing of the PoWs' march out of the camp

At 11 a.m., as usual, "Tommy's Bar" opened its shutters. Scarcely an hour later, it is said, on the point of midday, "an Italian bugler sounded three 'G's', the alarm call", writes Newby,[25] that meant "the Germans were on their way to take over the *orfanotrofio*". The prisoners headed down the stairs of the building but withdrew briefly while a German Ju 52 troop carrier flew low over the camp.[26]

The camp's evacuation was swift, orderly and decisive. Nobody was left behind, not even Newby who was handicapped by a broken ankle. Alongside the others, the young officer left the camp on the back of a mule provided by a *contadino*. Wearing military uniform and carrying sufficient rations for a day or two, the prisoners made sure they lost no time in proceeding to the exercise field where, in ranks and divided into their respective companies, they awaited further orders.

With the exception of some small work camps in northern Italy, "PG 49 was the only camp where the departure of prisoners of war was achieved in a completely organised and disciplined fashion".[27] The departure was rapid, taking barely ten minutes: the alarm was sounded at midday and by 12.10 PG 49 was empty.[*]

---

[*] The situation was different in the neighbouring camp, PG 55, at Busseto, less than 20 km away, and in its sub-camps beyond the left bank of the River Po. The inhabitants of these camps were almost exclusively Other Ranks: in June 1943 they numbered scarcely more than 750. The overwhelming majority were British, among whom there was just one officer (National Archives, London, WO 204/9732 and WO 224/178). The sub-camps were in fact agricultural businesses using the prisoners as workers: Ca' de' Fratti, Stagno Lombardo (PG 55/4) and Costa Sant'Abramo (PG 55/6). At the Armistice, according to British intelligence sources, PG 55 held about 500 prisoners. About 10–15 seem to have succeeded in escaping, while the "remainder [were] handed to Germans" (National Archives, WO 204/9732). Other information confirms "Camp 55 to be under German control", while "escapers report that prisoners in three sub-camps succeeded in escaping, and that another sub-camp was taken over by

Two years later, de Burgh published his own account of how the escape took place.

On 8 September [*sic*], 1943, at a prisoner of war camp in northern Italy, a British bugle call rang out suddenly – "The Alarm". It was repeated. For a moment all stood paralysed, then everyone was galvanised into sudden activity. This was the signal we had been waiting for. "The Alarm" had sounded at 12 noon. At 12.10 I passed through the gap where the wire had been cut, the last of six hundred British prisoners of war.

It sounds a curious thing that we "marched" out of a prison camp in an enemy country, but the Italian government was disintegrating and the Germans, who were in virtual occupation of the country, were moving all Allied prisoners to Germany. In view of this I and my staff had, with the aid of some of the Italian officers, organised the camp to be ready for some form of break-out, to avoid further imprisonment.

The reason for marching as we did in six companies was that I hoped that, if the Germans sent air or motor patrols to look for us, we,

---

Germans" (National Archives, WO 224/179). First-hand accounts are rare, although some PoW debriefing documents refer to successful escapes to Switzerland, as in the case of Edward Cormack. Together with eight prisoners, released by the sub-camp in which they found themselves on 9 September, he first gained refuge on a farm. Then, on 27 October, "when the farm was surrounded by Germans and all except Cormack were captured", he fled and succeeded in reaching the Swiss border (National Archives, WO 208/4246). The same happened with Frank Bell, who escaped from PG 55/4 on 10 September with a group of companions. Wearing civilian clothes, they reached Cremona, then Crema, Lecco, Bellano, Porlezza and finally a place above Lugano (National Archives, WO 208/4240).

marching across country through the trees and vines, would be mistaken for a German battalion. This was possible, as the German uniform might easily be mistaken for our own. Aeroplanes did fly low over us – and my gamble came off.[28]

Wanda Newby Skof was among those who witnessed the mass escape:

> A large number of villagers, including my father and me, went to watch the exodus of the prisoners, which was led by the senior British colonel. In their hundreds they set out calmly from the back of the building, through the exercise field towards the open country. Some were laughing, some talking, some silent. Among them was a young officer who was riding a mule (which stubbornly stopped from time to time) and roaring with laughter. I had seen him once before when he had waved to me from an upper window and I had waved back. Later I learned that he had injured his ankle running up and down stairs in the building in order to keep fit; the leg was very painful and he could not walk. None of us could imagine where the mule came from.[29]

The young officer became Wanda's husband in 1946.

Bell says that Major Ronnie Noble, "our own correspondent", recorded the whole evacuation.[30] Commandant Vicedomini had handed him back his camera shortly before the exodus. The news cameraman stood on the far side of the opening in the fence and took photographs of this exceptional mass escape. Unfortunately, the photos got lost along with others that he took in the following months.[31] While the men filed out of the camp in rows of three, saluted by Italian soldiers standing at attention, the thought that the Germans could arrive at any moment kept them all on tenterhooks. Carver was among the last to get out through the gap in the wire. Turning around, he gave a final glance at what had been the exercise field. It was deserted except for the four goslings, which had grown into geese thanks to the attentions of the guards who had fed them on lettuce and corn.[32]

The wedding of Eric and Wanda Newby, Santa Croce, Florence, April 1946

For months past, the prisoners had been obsessed with planning tunnels and conceiving improbable schemes of escape. Now they were leaving the camp through a hole in the wire made by the guards themselves.

On the outside, however, they would soon lose the sense of security that prison provided. They were free but disorientated and uncertain of what to do. They were anxious about what awaited them. Perhaps some were even scared. Many suffered from what became known in German prison camps as *"Gefangenitis"*, a feeling of apathy not far off from depression that afflicted those who spent too much time shut inside a camp.[33]

"It is a strange sensation to step into a landscape," recalls Hood. "For the last time we fell in in threes and then, a long straggling group, walked through the fence and into the fields. The watchtowers were empty. By the cemetery wall a couple of guards were siting a light machine gun to cover the entrance to the village."[34] Lt. Tony Davies remembers:

> We had seen the guards drop their weapons and run, and the villagers scuttle off into their houses and bar and bolt their doors, and from the panic, it was obvious the Germans were not far away. The villagers were under no illusions as to what the German mood would be when they discovered that the birds had flown, and so, very wisely, they were keeping out of sight.
>
> I felt very much happier once we had put a good quarter-of-an-hour's march between ourselves and the village. My sense of security increased as we penetrated deeper into the maze of rich cultivated farmland with its olive groves and cypresses.
>
> After some forty minutes' marching the column halted and dispersed in a grove of small stunted trees. Companies were well separated, and the whole "laager" area covered about a half-mile square. Through the middle ran a dry river bed, perhaps twenty feet wide and fifteen feet deep, and dotted with bushes.[35]

Kindersley recalls the hiding place clearly. "This was a small wood surrounded by a high grass bank and open stubble fields bordered by vines. The various companies were scattered under the vines, with headquarters company taking up a position in the wood. We were told that we should remain there until nightfall. Most of us took off our shirts, which were soaked with perspiration, and laid them out in the sun to dry. The first stage of our move had been accomplished without a hitch."[†] The order was to stay still and keep as quiet as possible, at least until sunset.

Settled in this rather insecure manner, the thing that most worried the fugitives was the fear of being betrayed. Lots of people – too many – knew of their hiding place. All that was needed was for a single guard to betray the escapers, or one of the townspeople who had watched or even accompanied them to their precarious refuge. If that happened, the escape concluded there and then. But, on the contrary, the local people made it their business in every way to protect and save the men from capture.

Hood, who spoke Italian fluently, and Captain Camino approached the houses nearby to get better information about what was happening. To increase the chances of not being discovered, they returned to their comrades dressed in civilian clothes lent by a *contadino* family. Changing out of uniform soon became popular among the fugitives.

Meanwhile, at about 3 p.m., a detachment of German soldiers had reached the camp. Commandant Vicedomini was waiting for them in his office. A rapid search of the building left no doubt about what had occurred; if any remained, then the hole in the wire was confirmation. Asking few questions, the German officer in command railed furiously at the Italian commandant. He accused him of treachery, and it seems he had him dragged outside with yells and kicks and put on a lorry. The destination was the Reich. Apparently there was also a suggestion he be shot on the spot in front of the local inhabitants, but this was rejected. Shooting an Italian officer in front of the people of

---

[†] Although Lt. Kindersley reports that the prisoners hid first in a small wood before transferring to the banks of the Rovacchia stream in Paroletta, which became known to the PoWs as the Bund, some accounts mention only the latter. Kindersley, pp. 72–73.

Fontanellato on the day of the Germans' arrival would not have been the best way of inaugurating the occupation.[36]

Vicedomini was deported to Mauthausen concentration camp, where despite privation and suffering he managed to survive. At the end of the war he returned to Italy in very poor health and, worn out by that terrible experience, he died in March 1946.[37] That year, Radio Tricolore recorded a tribute to him, recognising his "extreme heroism, profound sense of duty and noble simplicity with which he courageously faced up to his moral, human and military responsibilities".‡

In addition to Vicedomini, the German detachment took away Italian soldiers they discovered while combing the vicinity of the camp. One of these was Dario Fava of Fontanellato, at the time serving at Milan:

> On 7 September I was at Milan with the 3rd Regiment of *Bersaglieri*, with the role of courier. At the camp at Fontanellato the commandant was a colonel of the 30th *Bersaglieri* Regiment. That day I had to drive there with orders. So I asked my colonel: "Colonel, tomorrow there is the fair at Fontanellato, will you let me go by train so that I can stay at home tomorrow as well?" First, he said No, then he thought about it, got his adjutant to call me and told me: "Yes, go home by train and while there go to the cavalry barracks at Parma." So I said, "Give me somebody to accompany me", and he said, "Take anybody you want". I replied: "There is Rino Bettati, he comes from my village."
>
> So Bettati and I went to the station at Milan Lambrate and took the train, which came to a halt at Codogno, however. From the station we went to Via Emilia and got a lift in an empty Red Cross

---

‡ See Appendix 2.

vehicle that took us as far as Fidenza. From there I went to my sister's house, took a bicycle and arrived home.

On 9 September I caught a bus at Ghiare (a hamlet of Fontanellato) where I lived and left together with Bettati. But we didn't get as far as Parma. When we reached Fontevivo we were told there was fighting at Parma...so the bus turned back. At the *Santuario*, where the bus stopped, at the café, a sergeant and three soldiers climbed on. They made all the soldiers on the bus get off and go to the camp. [...] At 10.30–10.45 [*sic*], I believe, the order came, to let the English go free. Well, Piero Parella, one of the soldiers at the camp, cut the fence with wire cutters. There was a gate, but they cut the fence to save time. All the prisoners got out and behind them in formation went about 40 armed soldiers. I stayed in the camp. There were about 40 of us, some wanted to fight. There was a lieutenant, if I find him I don't know what I'll do to him, he said that the captain had given orders to resist...but I say they weren't even capable of using a machine gun, if they [the Germans] got in here they would kill us all. So everybody ran away.

Then the Germans arrived. When they saw the colonel, an SS lieutenant and Pietralunga, the interpreter, went up to the colonel and said: "Where are the prisoners?" "I was ordered to set them free," Vicedomini replied. As soon as he replied the lieutenant gave him a slap...then he removed the revolver from Vicedomini's belt and ordered his men to disarm all the soldiers. Meanwhile, I was thinking how I could escape. First I tried getting through the fence but a German sergeant spotted me and yelled at me to stop; everybody shouted at me "run, run", but it was too risky, for them too, a hail of bullets would also have hit them, so I turned back.

On a second attempt I tried where the *Carabinieri*'s and soldiers' barracks were; there was a little door that gave out on to the road to the cemetery. Seeing that it was open, my friend and I threw ourselves out of it. He went first but when it was my turn a captain saw me and started shouting "cowards, traitors, you're running away, eh". Rino Bettati had got through, I didn't make it...then came the German order to transfer us.[38]

Among the soldiers who avoided being rounded up was Romolo Bottoni (born 1910). On his return from the eastern border he had been transferred to PG 49 and given the role of interpreter. After fleeing from the camp before the Germans arrived, he reached Ca' Vernier in the Polesine area, where his family had taken refuge. He took part in the war of liberation as a member of the partisans of the Isola Di Ariano Polesine.[39]

Kindersley, from information he gathered after the war, says that

> two hours after we had evacuated Fontanellato, two German tanks and a company of infantry arrived to take over the camp. The Italian soldiers ran away, leaving the commandant to face the music. The Germans were furious at finding the building empty and gave vent to their feelings in a strange manner. They entered the building, drank all the wine they could lay their hands on, ate our cold lunch and then methodically smashed everything in the building. The drawers and cupboards were smashed with rifle butts; books, letters and papers were torn up and hurled, together with our clothes, out of the windows. They then loaded as many cigarettes and Red

Cross parcels as possible on to their trucks and sold the remainder, together with our clothes, to the civilian population. Officers who later returned to the camp to collect belongings after the Germans had gone reported an amazing spectacle of disorder.[40]

In fact, people from the village had already entered the camp in advance of the Germans. As mentioned, some reports have it that it was German soldiers who looted the prison after the prisoners got away. However, by the time the Germans arrived the building and stores had been explored by the locals, attracted especially by the provisions contained in the Red Cross parcels. They had convinced themselves while the camp operated that food, clothing, linen, soap, coffee – all luxuries the village lacked – were in the orphanage.

It was the luxuries from far away that fed the imagination of a populace ready to believe the camp lacked for nothing. Widespread looting of the deserted building by the inhabitants under the eyes of the Italian soldiers left on guard at PG 49 is, therefore, not surprising.

The stories of this sacking, coming directly from the perpetrators, cast the episode in the style of neorealism. "After the prisoners had left," says Wanda Newby Skof, "some boys, feeling rather brave, entered the building to see if there was anything left in it. No one seemed to be in charge of it. They brought out large packets of cigarettes – then rationed – and shared them out among the men who were on the road watching. My father could not believe his luck. For him, a heavy smoker, this was manna sent from heaven: he now had a large supply to keep him going."[41]

Ermes Arduini recalls:

Everybody from the village went there. We looted it because there was God-given stuff inside there. Going inside with the others, I looked for cigarettes. There was, I don't know, a kilo, a kilo and a half, or two…Then there was also coffee, chocolate, sugar, powdered milk. There was a bit of everything, you see, clothes, shoes, military stuff.

We, the village, that is, used to say: "look how lucky they are." They used to go out for walks a couple of times a week, inside there was every good thing possible…It's true that there were only a few civilians who had contact with the prisoners but we had used our imagination. I saw acts of heroism. They did the right thing, this was stuff that the Germans would have taken. It's true that the more cunning ones made money. However, I also saw women go out and chat with the guards and enable those of us who had helped the English to get away themselves. I saw people risk their own skin to help the next person.

The prisoners of war escaped with the help of the population. Already on 9 September we had at home a Slav and two English officers; then also an Italian soldier from a tank regiment at Fidenza, who had clashed with the Germans at Parma. He was a Sicilian, a motorcyclist. He too stayed a while, he got changed and then disappeared.[42]

Arduini continues:

Everybody was happily inside the orphanage picking up stuff but when the Germans arrived and started shooting they all disappeared. The Germans really did open fire, I saw them. They stayed there for a bit. Then, after the Germans had left, towards evening or when night had already fallen, I don't remember, people went back to take anything that was left.[43]

It was Camino who brought the news that German detachments had reached the camp about half an hour after the evacuation. Dressed in civilian clothes, he acted as go-between, shuttling from the village to the hiding place to update the fugitives; and to prepare them, as far as it was possible, for the next stage of the great escape.

In the wood, hundreds of men waited for dusk. Davies vividly remembers "the intense heat of the shimmering atmosphere". Lying in the shade under the trees he read that day's edition of the *Corriere della Sera*. "Blazoned across the front page in four-inch black lettering was the one word '*Armistizio*'."[44]

Eric Newby recalls how, "below one of the steep, grassy embankments, we lay down under the vines and waited, dozing and discussing the various rumours that came to us, no one seemed to know from where".[45]

After four hours crouching in the vegetation, some of the men became restless. A Junkers aircraft again flew low over the area, searching for the servicemen, while military vehicles drove around the country lanes looking for anything that might indicate their presence.

Bell recalls the anxiety prompted by one enemy vehicle that stopped a short distance from where he was taking cover. Getting out of the vehicle, German soldiers approached a farmhouse near the former prisoners' hiding place:

> All the family were brought out in front of the house and were carefully questioned. The Germans seemed to spend more time on the children. Although the voices were clear I had difficulty in understanding what was going on. By their actions and facial expressions we gathered that the Germans were unable to find what they were looking for. Without searching the farm, they jumped on to their truck and headed back the

way they had come, smashing down the family's
maize and other crops in the process.[46]

When night fell at last, de Burgh gave the order to
transfer to the Rovacchia embankment, or Bund. The men
found room beneath the embankment and in the adjoining
maize field, while the Senior British Officer and his staff
took up their position in a neighbouring wood.[47]

A section of the Bund (Rovacchia stream), photographed in 2018. In
September 1943, when 600 PoWs took refuge here, it was more overgrown,
with maize and vines planted in the adjacent fields

The decision to move all the escapers, both the officers
and Other Ranks, to the Bund was undoubtedly taken for
logistical reasons: the water course made it easier to conceal
such a large number of men; it provided vegetation and there
were farms nearby that were sufficiently off the beaten track;
and enemy detachments were unlikely to pass by that way by
chance. The place had been earmarked during the weekly
walks and chosen as the refuge by Mainwaring during his

inspection. Sandro Baruffini, then aged 11, confirms: "They chose the Bund for this reason: once or twice a week we used to see them while we were working in the fields. They would march, that is, they took exercise in formation. They always came that way. It was a little further away from Via Emilia, further away from the route taken by the Germans. There was less traffic and it was therefore less monitored, unlike the other side in the direction of Parma."[48]

The new hiding place was baptised the "*Quartiere della Macchia*" (Bush Quarters) by the local people. The "*Quartiere Generale*" (Headquarters), comprising Colonels de Burgh, Lee and Tyndale-Biscoe, together with Reggie Phillips, Camino and his assistant Paride Paini, was installed in the home of the Merli family.[49]

Lt. Col. Denis L. A. Gibbs describes what it was like to spend that first night in the open.

> Thus we settled down for the night, a bright moonlit night, and here for the first time since our capture we were out in it, in the open air! There were no barbed wire or arc lamps to look at; no raised sentry platforms at the corners of the wire enclosures manned by Breda machine guns, no shouting of Italian soldiery. The nights in the camp were seldom quiet – soldiers singing [on their way] home from the village, soldiers disputing as only Italians can dispute, sentries clearing their throats and spitting in that familiar Latin manner, and the tramp and clatter of the night duty officer and his minions as he went his rounds, two or three times nightly, along the stone passages and up and down the stone stairs of our "home", the orphanage, and the click and sudden flare-up of light as he switched on the room lights to count heads.
>
> There was none of that but instead this night was moonlit and quiet with the tranquil night

sounds – crickets, frogs and nightjars and, through windows in the scrub and trees, I could see long rows of vines outlined against the moon and, beyond, a monster poplar standing majestically.

Yet such pleasant reveries were short-lived, being cut short not by any Germans but by an army of mosquitoes whose sluggish riverbed had never before presented them with so luscious a morsel as our unprotected bodies must have offered. I could only snatch a little sleep by swathing my face in my towel, wearing my hat and tucking my hands underneath my coat. I can hear the "humming" of those mosquitoes and experience again, in my mind, the low-level stinging attacks upon me, time after time, like German Air Force Dive Bombs in the retreat to Dunkirk![50]

Few managed to sleep during that long night in the Bund. Mosquitoes and the fear of being discovered kept many awake. The hope that the Allies would rapidly advance was not completely abandoned, even though the surrounding countryside was filling up with Germans. Many of the former detainees were still inclined to believe wild but persistent rumours that there would definitely be new Anglo-American landings at La Spezia, Genoa or Trieste.[51]

During their stay, both in the small wood and then along the Bund, the officers received innumerable visits from the locals. Some brought food, clothing or money; others gave advice and tips about the next stage of the escape. "We went up to where the English prisoners were hiding," relates Rino Casalini. "One of them told us 'go to the camp and get those tins'. Blimey, those tins were full of things we wouldn't possibly have – no way: milk powder, as many tins of pork as you wanted, cigarettes and 'tobacco' [laughter], soon the whole town was smoking tea! In particular, I took away a box of shoes; there were a dozen pairs in each box. There was a room full of soldiers' boots. I took one, and when my father got back home they arrested him for having assisted the English; he had swapped boots for wheat."[52]

Despite constant warnings from the former prisoners' headquarters, Fontanellato's citizens trekked to the Bund to take food and clothing. This, of course, amazed the British officers. Bell remarks: "The *contadini*...were now being extremely co-operative."[53] For as long as the fugitives remained at the Bund the Italians persevered with their laudable task of patrolling the surrounding roads to ensure the Germans did not spring a surprise. Another objective was to restore to the servicemen the contents of the Red Cross parcels that remained in the camp. Bell says: "Tins of condensed milk were brought along, together with cocoa, sugar, bully beef, etc., which they could have kept for their own under-nourished children. Even the children came out with their pockets and bags full of cigarettes and tobacco."[54]

Going to greet the former prisoners, taking them clothes and food, became a collective effort – something that ended up involving much of the population of Fontanellato. Perhaps, too, it was a way of exorcising fear, a rite that succeeded in strengthening bonds within the community at a time of great uncertainty and unfavourable omens. According to Kindersley, "all the Italians in the district must have known where we were, and it says a lot for their loyalty to us that no one betrayed us to the Germans".[55]

The officers were getting a bit restless, anxious to be on the move. However, de Burgh was adamant: everybody would stay where they were until the manhunt conducted by the Germans had lost a little of its intensity. Military vehicles were everywhere, but, as the hours went by, the chances of not being discovered improved. This, above all, was because the Germans expanded the radius of the search in the belief that the escapers could not still be just a few kilometres from the camp.

On average, the soldiers remained hidden at the Bund for one night and one day. Kindersley talks of "the longest [day] I have ever spent"[56] with no possibility at any stage of trying his luck outside the refuge because of the number of Germans on the move. Aware that he would not be able to keep his men hidden there for long, de Burgh changed his original plan and gave permission to three companies (one of which was the orderly company) to set off during the night of 10/11 September, cross the Via Emilia, break into small parties and attempt to reach the hills. During that night several other officers went off in small groups, some seeking hospitality at the farms nearest the Bund. However, the majority of those in the remaining companies obeyed de Burgh's instruction to stay put, postponing departure until the following day.

The farmhouse at Soragna, near Fontanellato, where Dan Billany and David Dowie were sheltered by Dino Meletti immediately after their escape from PG 49

At last came the order to disperse. By the night of 11/12 September those who were still there had split into groups of two, or at most three, and left the hiding place in a hurry.

Scarcely 20 or so chose to stay in the encampment area and wait for the situation to clarify.[57] Some spent a week or more near the Bund in the homes of *contadini* while they decided whether to proceed towards the Apennines or attempt to cross over the Alps to Switzerland.[58]

Most opted for the former: the Po valley and river were extremely risky obstacles. Besides, once the men reached Switzerland they would be interned again; the Apennines and freedom were more attractive for many. From these mountains they could reach the Gulf of Genoa where an Allied landing was possible, or travel along the ridges and meet the forces advancing up Italy.

The thought that it might be worthwhile remaining in the area sprang from the belief, still common among the former prisoners, that the Allies would not take long to reach the Po valley. Perhaps, ran this argument, it was a good idea to hide among the *contadini* on the plain and in the Apennines to await their comrades. Kindersley was keen to leave:

> The plan was to hide up in the Apennines until the Allies had completed the job – probably a matter of about 10 days. We were all, I think, immensely relieved to be going, as the strain of hiding so close to the Germans was beginning to tell. Luckily the company to which I belonged was scheduled to move that night as soon as it was dark.
>
> Before our departure we had one disturbing scare. At six o'clock we were sitting in the bushes smoking cigarettes and discussing plans when a terrified Italian sergeant arrived and told us that the *Tedeschi* (Germans) were coming. It looked as though the game was up. However, it proved to be a false alarm. A platoon of German infantry had passed down the road but, little suspecting

that 600 English soldiers were just around the corner, they continued on their way.[59]§

During the evening of 11 September the Bund's embankment lost most of its remaining occupants. At this point the story of one of the biggest escapes in Italy during the Second World War fragments into hundreds of different tales. Although these have a common theme, they developed with a multitude of variations – each of which had a bearing on the escaper's progress and eventual outcome. Many of the stories have reached us through the soldiers' diaries, preserved at the Imperial War Museum in London and narrated in numerous publications since the war. Captain Williams writes:

> We had soon discovered that concealment in Italy was next to impossible. Wherever we went the farmers and shepherds sniffed us out from the woods or hedges. We always looked utterly English, no matter how we tried: whether it was our general appearance, our borrowed clothes, our bearing or our Saxon complexions, we never fully discovered, and few of us managed to hoodwink intelligent Italians for long. Eventually we more or less gave it up and trusted to Providence.[60]

---

§ From the Bund, Lt. Kindersley went to a village near Bardi in the Apennines where he stayed for seven weeks and resumed writing. His first manuscript had been left behind at Fontanellato. He then went south and was captured by a Fascist unit between Gubbio and Perugia. Forced to jettison his notebooks during the hunt, so as not to compromise his helpers, he began to write again only when he reached his new prison camp, Oflag V111F at Märisch Trubau (Moraskvá Třebová in the Czech Republic). He returned to England at the end of the war.

Some of the Italian soldiers who had taken part in preparations for the escape threw in their lot with the former prisoners. Among them was Camino, from Caluso in the Aosta valley, who at the orphanage had acted as interpreter and was Commandant Vicedomini's right-hand man. In his escape report, de Burgh describes Camino as "very pro-British", with business interests in Slough and an English wife. He says Camino "worked very hard to obtain civilian clothes for over 300 of us. Also got villagers and farmers to bring food. Provided money."[61] Lt. Prevedini and Sergeant Major Carlo Rissotto also stayed with the former prisoners.

When everybody had set off, Camino offered to guide de Burgh, Lt. Col. Wheeler and Captain Phillips to the Aosta valley, from where they could attempt to climb over the Alps to Switzerland. They reached the valley via Milan, where they spent the night in a bomb-damaged house that belonged to Remo Gandini, of Fontanellato, who had accompanied them. At Champoluc in the Ayas valley, which branches off from the Aosta valley, they first organised passage over the border for some soldiers who had come from the plain – mainly New Zealanders. Then they themselves got over to Swiss territory, Wheeler going separately. In three days de Burgh and Phillips climbed over the Lyskamm Pass, at 4,565 metres, and descended to Zermatt.[62]**

Meanwhile, the Germans had occupied all the railway stations around Fontanellato in an attempt to catch at least some of the 600 ex-prisoners in hiding. The former detainees of PG 49 came across a huge number of people on the roads leading to freedom; many helped the British soldiers, saving them from capture and assisting them as they pushed on towards home. For most of the escapers the aim, ambitious

---

** After his return to service, Lt. Col. de Burgh was in command of the Allied Screening Commission (Italy), which was responsible for giving recognition to, and compensating, those who had assisted Allied personnel behind enemy lines following the Armistice.

though it seemed, was to be "home by Christmas".[63] Several succeeded.

Williams says:

> We found the majority of families extremely friendly, though many were frightened. Every village, and often every house in it, had people who had been in America or the UK. Failing that, someone always had a relative there, who was sure to have been a coal miner, fruit farmer, ice-cream vendor, waiter or mosaic worker.
>
> They did have some reason for their fears, though. We know that the Blackshirts were more barbarous and inhumane even than the Germans, and many a scorched village bore testimony to their ferocity. Priests were their special mark, and several were tortured and shot in public for supposed or actual assistance to the English or the partisans.
>
> At about sundown one of us would approach a village or lone house and ask for some food and somewhere to sleep. Often this met with a blank refusal. We normally found that the richer the house the poorer was its hospitality, so finally we only asked the poorest, though sometimes we tried as many as six houses before someone took pity on us. Our bed was usually hay in a barn, or dry leaves collected for cows' bedding. The leaves were chestnut (prickles included), but far warmer for bedding than hay or straw, so we did not grumble.[64]

Captain Carol Mather and Lt. Archie Hubbard chose to climb over the Apennines to reach the Ligurian coast, where an Allied landing was believed to be imminent. They walked at night, crossing the Via Emilia at Parola and aiming for the mountain range. For them and others, going beyond the Via

Emilia, which the former prisoners saw as an extremely dangerous obstacle, was like abandoning the modern world to enter the past: a poor world of long ago, yet to be visited by progress.

The risk of bumping into German patrols, however, was a problem that belonged to the present. Also of the present was the chance, from time to time, to listen to BBC broadcasts in the houses of the fugitives' hosts. It was on one such occasion that Mather and his companion learned there had not been a landing at La Spezia or anywhere near and that the Allies still found themselves hundreds of kilometres away in south Italy. Mather and the many others who had reached the Apennines faced nothing other than a "long walk home" towards the south if they wished to regain the liberty they so dearly desired before Christmas.[65]

Captain Carol Mather dressed as a contadino, *photographed after he reached the Allied lines on 17 October 1943*

3. The Population

In the days that followed the escape from PG 49 at Fontanellato "the Italian community was most helpful", says Phillip Kindersley.[1] Lt. Col. de Burgh was to write later: "We hid, concentrated in good cover, for two nights, during which time the Italian peasants brought us food and civilian clothing, thus enabling most of us to melt away in small parties in various directions. The majority of the 600 got back either to our own forces or to Switzerland."[2]

Giuseppe Sambataro, a Fontanellato doctor, anti-Fascist and member of the clandestine Resistance movement, described the population's behaviour as "an outburst of generosity from a village that Fascist propaganda had never succeeded in enslaving to the German idol; nor had the propaganda succeeded in making it hate the English. It was a genuine outburst from a village that had never wanted the German war, nor enthused about it, and which exploded, as soon as possible, in demonstrations of affection towards the English officers and co-operation with them. This was done with a will that was truly admirable."[3]

By 5 p.m. of the day following the flight, nearly 200 prisoners had been fitted out in civilian clothes and arrangements made for them to be sheltered by the local *contadini*. Sambataro says: "*Commendatore* Paolo Scerni, at our urging, was the first to take in and look after 14 prisoners. His example was immediately followed by those nearest, and then by those further away, and then by the neighbouring communities of Soragna, San Secondo, Fontevivo... Something that had seemed impossible on the morning of 10 September had become a reality by 16 September."[4]

Kindersley reports: "The local girls were most helpful and seemed to be enjoying the situation thoroughly. In one case, three of them arrived at our hideout with an Italian man and two sets of civilian clothes. Two officers changed into the clothes and then walked back in daylight arm-in-arm with a girl apiece, as if returning from an afternoon's stroll."[5]

"One came across them [the girls] everywhere," says Sambataro, "and they always used to smile at you as if to say 'have you noticed that we too are doing our best?'"[6]

The assistance given to Allied servicemen was in line with the strong show of support made by the lion's share of the Italian population on behalf of all the disbanded people roaming the country in their attempts to avoid capture and return home. These included Italian soldiers coming from France or Yugoslavia, or simply from barracks within Italy's borders; foreign citizens seeking to slip secretly out of Italy; military prisoners; civilian internees; Italian and foreign Jews; and anti-Fascists on the wanted list. All were looking for a way to evade the German army; all needed help and support, which they found by knocking on doors in towns as well as in the countryside.

As shown by the case of Fontanellato, rescue was not merely a feminine prerogative. The whole population gave succour to disbanded soldiers. It was not purely an instance of *maternage*,[7] as female historians have frequently stressed, but also of *paternage*. It was not only the women who saw their own sons in the persons of the young Italian or Allied soldiers on the run; men, too, were affected by the same sentiments. For them, the fugitives were their sons dispersed on the Front Lines.

It was in this spirit that the family of Andrea Baruffini offered hospitality, although Andrea himself was to pay heavily for it, as we shall see in Chapter Six. His sons tell the story:

> They came on their own, they knocked on everybody's door; let me say, when we understood that 8 September was not the end of the war but the start of another, the saddest one, anybody with humanity said, "that's enough, let's help the Italians, let's help prisoners". Because we

are not Germans. So my poor dad who had fought against them in '15–'18…he couldn't stand them, that's the thing. The majority of the people of Fontanellato got down to it. They helped the prisoners and soldiers, they clothed them, fed them. I always remember when we opened our door and three prisoners from the orphanage came in, my dad said to my mum: "We've got three male children, there will always be war, Luigina, I suggest you look after them well!"[8]

Ermes Arduini says: "I went down to the Bund [the name given by the prisoners to the bank of the Rovacchia stream] with my mother. They had escaped with absolutely nothing and we took them a few things which, of course, we had removed from the orphanage."[9]

But not everything came from the prison camp's store. "Seven hundred bread rations provided by the bakers Incerti and Maccagnoni were carried down to the Bush headquarters, while dairy farmer Ricardo Abrati, at Sambataro's request, put five quintals of milk at the disposition of the prisoners."[10]

Bruno Gotti recalls: "An Englishman and an American came to my house, through Signora Gelati, a Fontanellato employee; they had built a kind of shelter, I'd helped them, on the reclaimed canal, the Re brook, under a low tree, a bush. They had turned it into a kind of cave, they used to go and hide there if something happened. They spent the day there but also in the fields with us, cutting beet, for example. They would eat with us and they also had their room."[11]

Bruna Chiappini, who married Gotti, recalls:

Something my mother-in-law always told me is that they didn't eat horse. One evening he was given horse-meat balls and after he had eaten them she asked: "Well, Gianni, are they good?" "Yes, very good," he replied. "What are they?"

"It's horse..." [laughter]... and he was amazed... well, you know, they don't eat horse where he comes from.

And at Torchio, a hamlet between Fontevivo and Castelguelfo, there was a midwife who had taken in an Englishman who knew barely three or four words in Italian. One day the Germans arrived, pitched a machine gun in front of her home and searched all the houses. She was worried and told the Englishman, "be careful, the Germans are here", and then she felt ill and withdrew. However, he opened the door. "Come in, make yourselves comfortable..." as if there was nothing to worry about. They had a good look around and then went away. After that the Englishman went up to the mountains...but it seems that he had trouble there too because of spies.[12]

Eric Newby, limping because of his injured ankle, found shelter in a loft with a family whose farm was near the Bund:

> When it grew dark the farmer, whose name was Merli, came up the ladder and signed to me to come down. I was glad to get out of the *fienile*, the loft, although my hay fever had gone at last. His wife was dark and pale and slight. The two children were beautiful, miniature editions of their mother. They were all curious about my uniform, the whipcord trousers, the battledress jacket with the polished brass pips, my silk muffler and my one beautiful new boot (the other was in my pack). Like everyone else, I was wearing my best clothes, wanting to appear decent when our own troops arrived. She fed me on *pasta asciutta*, and what she called *grana*, what I called Parmesan.[13]

Following that, Newby spent a short time in the hospital at Fontanellato before he too took refuge in the mountains. There, however, he was to be captured and sent to Germany.[14]

Many of the witness statements record tales of prisoners who cocked a snook at the Germans, such as this one from Gotti. Referring to *Il Moro* – meaning the dark-haired Englishman whom he had put up in his house – Gotti says that "he came to Fontanellato on Sundays with my brother-in-law, Attilio Marocchi. He used to hang around in the square as if it were his own home."[15]

Another witness was Giuseppe Azzali:

In September we were immediately brought two English officers. They were nice people. They used to eat with us at home, morning, midday and in the evening. At first they didn't want to come in but we insisted, and we got them used to coming to us in the house. They used to sleep in a ditch at the back where there was a little wood, they had put up planks and made the ditch into a hut. There used to be lots of trees and vine rows there, not like now, and it wasn't so difficult to hide oneself. They used to sleep there, read a lot, and come to the house to eat.

To pass the time – they had never worked because they had studied, they were officers – as I say, to pass the time when they were in the orphanage they had dug a field. They had asked for a spade and a piece of land to exercise on, to keep fit. And so they got blisters on their hands…[laughter]…you could certainly see that they had never done any work. What always worried them was that they didn't know how they could reciprocate. They stayed here about 40 days but we never gave any thought to that, also because we all used to eat together, just like

home…Many of the prisoners went up into the
mountains but they didn't want to go there
because they were already old: two elderly
officers, I don't know if they were majors,
anyway, officers, and they didn't wish to go away
again. They said: "We'll stay here even if the
Germans arrive, they can do what they want." It
was as if they were resigned.

Then the Germans carried out a raid. That
morning I was seeing to the cattle, I remember I
was in the cowshed early because my father was
ill in bed. They [the officers] knew that and that
morning as they had seen the light on they came
over to the cowshed to ask how my father was
and to help me. They were really good people,
extremely decent! That morning the Germans
came; just think, if they had come another
morning they wouldn't have found them, they
happened to do it exactly when the prisoners were
there. However, they knew there were two of
them. Many of the prisoners had already joined
the partisans in the mountains, the Germans knew
that two had remained with us. It's certain they
took them to Germany and I don't know what
happened to them. I do know that they were very
fond of me and they were always telling me:
"When we go home we'll come and get you and
you will come to England with us." But I never
heard anything more, who knows if they returned
from Germany.[16]

In her account, Renata Avanzini says:

They used to go to the houses near the Bund. At
the time they would knock on doors of all the
homes, even the Fascists', and these too ended up
holding them. Near our house at the time there

was a tree. They dug a hole around it, surrounded
it with stakes and hid themselves inside. My
mother and aunts took them food in the evenings.
They stayed there for a bit...I can't remember
now exactly how long, only that after a time the
Germans began searching and they started saying:
"If we stay on here it's going to be bad for you,"
and things like that. So they asked me for dye for
their uniforms, but that wasn't so easy to find
then. Eventually I found some and dyed the
uniforms black, ironed them and handed them
back. And they said: "Now we're proper
Fascists!"[17]

In their testimony after the war, Andrea Baruffini's sons
say:

They [the prisoners] soon became part of the
population because people were tired of the war.
People felt relaxed because previously at
Fontanellato we hadn't suffered big disasters
during the war. After 8 September, though, when
the Germans arrived, people became exasperated
and grew increasingly weary of the war, fed up
with this life of food rationing and so on. I
remember that we didn't have any more clothes
in our homes, we'd given so many away so that
they [the prisoners] wouldn't be recognised. They
moved around at night and during the day they
slept in the barns and in the Rovacchia [the Bund].
They covered little creeks with freshly cut
branches so as not to be seen. Then the Germans
issued a proclamation: anybody holding English
prisoners was obliged to denounce them. After a
few days came the first round-up and I remember
it well, my poor father told me: "Go and destroy
all the shelters," but our prisoners had already left,

three reached Switzerland and one got captured, which was bad luck for my father.[18]

Not everybody was fortunate enough to find a welcome near the Bund, as this anonymous prisoner reports:

> I soon decided that the crowd was too big so I nudged LW and went over the bank and LW followed. Shortly after larking around in the dark on the other side we saw a pair of white trousers walking across the field and a closer inspection proved them to belong to JB. We three decided that the thing to do was get our heads down somewhere. So we walked on a bit and after five or ten minutes saw a dim light through the grape vines. JB volunteered to investigate so LW and myself waited under the vines. After what seemed an hour but was only about ten minutes, the pair of white trousers came walking out of the darkness once again.
>
> He reported that the light came from a cow stall inside of which three South Africans, GL and the VG brothers, were consulting maps torn from an ordinary school atlas. None of them turned out to be much good. We decided to go in and have a look, and it was here that I first regretted not having learned Italian. The South African GL seemed to manage all right, JB managed with a struggle to make himself understood but the VG brothers, LW and myself were starting from scratch. We messed about in this stall for a time getting nowhere but when GL asked the *contadino* if we could sleep in his barn, he refused and said something about the Germans concentrating 40 divisions in Italy and that it was too dangerous. We learned afterwards that he had been a big Fascist.[19]

Prisoners were also put up in houses in the village near the castle of Rocca Sanvitale. "On about 15 September the Germans returned to search for prisoners still hidden in the area," says Arduini. "First they went to the convent, then to Gandini's garden, which they went over metre by metre. Pietro was there, the gardener who had got the prisoners out through a small door there, just in time."[20]

Rino Casalini, whose home sheltered several fugitives, relates:

> We had two English officers. I lived in the corner of the village where there is a big vault above the shop. On 9 September a friend and I followed them to the Rovacchia stream [the Bund]. You know, at the time I was 15 years old and we saw these Englishmen who used to march – but that is something of a Fontanellato story, a story everybody can tell. Well, here, at the time, there was a kind of euphoria, about how the English and American forces would move up the country in 24 hours. Instead that wasn't the case, but the leading Fascists kept their distance in order to lie low for the time being.
>
> These Englishmen, for the first few days they got on as best they could, hiding themselves under the trees, eating the food they had taken with them, but in a short time they didn't have any left. That was when committees formed to collect things from the camp and then came the moment when it became necessary to take them into homes; this was suggested and one couldn't say No. In October, after staying for about a month, many began to leave the homes. The smartest among them had already reached Switzerland some time ago. Many stayed here, while others went into the mountains, but it seems only a few joined the partisans.

Rocca Sanvitale in Fontanellato

My father [Cornelio] thought up a way of sending them away. There was a naval officer who had escaped from La Spezia who, before fleeing, had, however, hidden a boat. He [my father] talked to the prisoners about it and organised the journey to La Spezia: a man called Arduini, who was a driver, accompanied them to Parma and from there to La Spezia by train. But the boat was no longer there, obviously. So they turned back and returned to our house.

Then rumours started up: these were caught, that other was captured, and you could see that my father was worried. On 23 November, Rossi warned us: "Look, the Germans are coming!" They appeared, picked up my father and took him to Parma and shut him up in the *Cittadella*. He was interrogated and beaten but he didn't talk. The Germans would have let him go after two or three days, basically because they hadn't discovered any Englishmen in our house and because they had other problems to think about. However, the

Italian court refused and so transferred him to Castelfranco Emilia.[21]

Following that, Cornelio Casalini was put on a list to be shot at Modena in reprisal, but as luck would have it everything got put off at the last moment. Meanwhile, his wife had also been arrested. Both of them returned to Fontanellato between 7 October and 9 October 1944.[22]

The soldiers remaining on the plain were still running many risks, but even greater ones confronted the population. Threats were followed by proclamations against anybody who assisted the former prisoners.

A terse British intelligence report runs: "Italians generally less likely to help since German Proclamation offering rewards, threatening death for harbouring. Civilians in [*illegible*] hypnotised by German occupation methods and severe penalties. Helpers terrified, inactive; Fascists denouncing them. No confidence Badoglio as run away [from Rome to Brindisi]."*

A large proportion of those who were still hiding in the countryside began to desert the plain to reach the Swiss border, attempt to rejoin the Allies, or hide in the mountains. There they would take advantage of the hospitality of the *contadini* or throw in their lot with the partisan bands that were springing up.

---

* On 8 September 1943 Marshal Pietro Badoglio, who had been appointed prime minister by King Vittorio Emanuele in July 1943 after the fall of Benito Mussolini, fled with his government and the Royal family from Rome to Brindisi. National Archives, London, WO 204/9732.

4. The Resistance

Official British reports tend to emphasise the civilian population's big contribution to the prisoners' cause while overlooking, if not dismissing, the part played by the emerging political entities of the Parma region's Resistance movement. The focus of attention is the population's spontaneous outburst and the prisoners' collaboration with the soldiers in Camp PG 49 who supported the government of Marshal Badoglio. The role of the underground movement in assisting the escapers, at first in the countryside around Fontanellato and then in the Apennines, is liable to remain in the shadows, mainly because of the dearth of documentary evidence.

Without detracting from the courage shown by the population, the contributions of the *Comitato di Liberazione Nazionale Alt'Italia* (CLNAI), as the CLN was known in north Italy, the Parma region's *Comitato di Liberazione* and the local *comitati* (committees) should be mentioned.* This is not

---

* The task of organising assistance to Allied prisoners of war was entrusted to Giuseppe Bacciagaluppi by Ferruccio Parri, a prominent member of the Resistance movement's Comitato di Liberazione Nazionale (CLN), in agreement with other anti-fascist groups. Parri was aware of the Allies' concern for the fate of the former prisoners who were at large in the countryside of north and central Italy after 8 September. Bacciagaluppi writes that Parri, "realising that it was incumbent on the CLN's military command to take over from the Rome government, which was completely powerless to carry out its obligation under the Armistice to provide help, decided to set up a CLN service to assist Allied prisoners of war". The tasks of the service were to: help prisoners reach Switzerland, Allied troops or partisan units; supply prisoners who found it impossible to move from their places of hiding; and contact individuals and groups with the means to give donations or practical help. The CLN of Milan was in charge of these duties, assisted by local CLNs and private citizens. It paid expenses to "professional guides (smugglers)", at 100 lire a time, for obtaining bicycles, rowing boats (to cross Lake Como) and the various kinds

merely for the sake of telling the whole story and giving credit to the men of the CLN, but also because their timely intervention had political and military consequences. The CLN's involvement, not only with the Allied soldiers but also with all the disbanded personnel roaming the countryside, was aimed at collecting weapons and saving those who had left their units and prisons from being captured by the Germans. The initiative had effects that would become apparent later.

First, the need to identify secure hiding places led to the establishment of safe houses on the Po plain and in the mountains that turned out to be indispensable in the course of Italy's liberation struggle. But the most significant political effect was to channel the people's humanitarian instincts – and the opposition to war that this presupposed – into open support of the Resistance movement. The help given to the Allied soldiers in the villages of the plain and the Apennines reflected an about-turn of the people's attitude to one in favour of the former enemy – a switch that had a big impact on the development of the armed struggle.

It became evident from the passage of countless prisoners through the valleys of the Stirone, the Ceno and the Taro that the inhabitants had a great deal more in

---

of transport used for getting to the frontier. Specific "passages" were organised for prisoners depending on which region of Italy they came from: for those who came from the Emilia camps, the route involved crossing the lower end of Lake Como. In total, between September 1943 and March 1945, the CLN organisation helped 1,865 former prisoners cross the Swiss border (1,297 British, 313 Slavs, 255 others). (Giuseppe Bacciagaluppi, *L'aiuto del Comitato di liberazione nazionale ai prigionieri di guerra alleati*, in Federazione Italiana Associazioni Partigiane – Fiap, Special Force Club, *N. 1 Special Force nella Resistenza italiana*, volume 1. Bologna: Clueb, 1990, pp. 203–11.) More information on work carried out by Bacciagaluppi can be found in Roger Absalom (1991), *A Strange Alliance: Aspects of Escape and Survival in Italy 1943–1945*. Florence: Accademia Toscana di Scienze e Lettere "La Colombaria", pp. 39 ff.

common with the British than with the Germans. There had been emigrants to Great Britain from those areas for decades, and many British soldiers were astonished to hear the frequent greeting of "Good morning" from the *contadini* they encountered on the mountain paths.

A plaque erected by the people of Fontanellato in 1983 in commemoration of the Allied prisoners of war and the Italians who helped them.

"In memory on the fortieth anniversary of the English and Allied prisoners of war interned here at PG 49 concentration camp and of the population of Fontanellato which after the Armistice of 8 September 1943 helped and hid them at the risk of harsh reprisals Fontanellato 11 September 1983"

This contact not only nourished the pro-Allies sentiment but also influenced subsequent attitudes towards the partisan bands. But that is another story. Given the shortage of available records, the issue of interest is how to clarify the role that the first CLN in the Parma region played in supporting the former prisoners. Of help here are some important written statements, which do not exhaust the subject but certainly open avenues of research.

Vittorio Skof as a young man

In the days immediately after the Armistice, the leaders of Parma's CLN were at Fontanellato to establish contact both with the area's anti-Fascists – Vittorio Skof and Giuseppe Sambataro the chief among them – and with representatives of the former prisoners. Skof was a Slovenian schoolteacher whose nationality was Italian because parts of Slovenia had been ceded to Italy after 1918. As was the case with many state employees of Slav origin during the Fascist regime, he was transferred far away from his homeland, arriving in Fontanellato with his family in 1932. Wanda, the teacher's daughter, remembers her father's friendship with Sambataro and the latter's anti-fascist feelings.

He was supported in his anti-fascist beliefs by his great friend the local general practitioner, Dr.

Sambataro, who lived in Fontanellato. A tall, very intelligent, rather bear-like man, and a Sicilian by birth, the doctor was highly regarded by his colleagues and patients alike. Like my father he did not suffer fools gladly, and he had an air of considerable authority which belied his great kindness. Because of his standing in the village he ventured at times to talk in a way which later proved disastrous about his anti-fascist feelings.[1]

Both men were arrested in October 1943: Skof succeeded in regaining his freedom, while the doctor, feigning an attack of appendicitis, was taken to hospital, from where he fled to the mountains to find refuge among the partisan bands.[2]

Tonino Chiari, a member of the *Fronte della Gioventù* (youth section) in the Parma region, was sent to Fontanellato at the appropriate moment to establish contact with the escapers. He relates:

On 12 or 13 September a courier from Fontanellato brought the news that hundreds of officers who had been prisoners of war (American, English, Canadian, Slav, etc.) were concealed in that area; their situation was serious and unsustainable. Most of them had come from the North African battlefields and they had escaped from the local concentration camp on 8 September [*sic*]. They wished to be put in touch with the Italian Resistance organisation. The Salsomaggiore area group decided to take action.

Accompanied by the courier I went to Fontanellato to carry out an immediate check and to ascertain the exact position so as to make an accurate report, and also to give an account of the expected presence of Germans and the probable intervention of local Fascists, who were already under our eye. The roads near the village were all but deserted; only a German armoured car was driving around with its guns levelled. Tension was evident in the centre of the village. A courageous signorina (Benita), doing an excellent job, set up an immediate meeting with a Canadian lieutenant and a British captain. Despite language difficulties, the situation seemed clear and it was possible to make an objective report.

At Parma, [Dante] Gorreri personally ordered me to go to an appointed place and meet a "certain person" who was authorised to confer with representatives of the men on the loose. After linking up with Salsomaggiore, I went to the place agreed upon: the "certain person" arrived punctually, namely the engineer Giacomo Ferrari, one of the chiefs of the active Resistance movement. The delegation that was authorised to consult our representative consisted of four soldiers, bearing the rank and uniform of their respective armies. A fifth officer, a British naval doctor, acted as interpreter. It was a positive meeting in that it clarified all the facts necessary for making subsequent decisions. It ended with Ferrari promising to give definitive information.

Afterwards, in fact, as ordered, I let the foreign delegation know that it had been decided to offer them unconditional assistance for their move to the Apennines; more precisely, towards Bardi. Escorted by our units, and with the admirable participation of the population, the trek towards the Bardi area began that night, following a nearby river upstream. Each group, together with our guides, got past the many crucial points, despite the reported presence of motorised German detachments patrolling the Pellegrino-

Salsomaggiore zone. There wasn't a single loss, there were no informers and no sabotage.

As a priority – following Gorreri's instructions – I escorted the first foreign officer to Bardi, via Varrone, Pellegrino, Bore. That was in line with commitments made at Fontanellato with Ferrari and was so that the Canadian could prepare for the arrival of his comrades, as then duly happened. As was expected, along the way we repeatedly came across German motorcycle gunners. The personal mission with which I had been entrusted by Dante Gorreri and Giacomo Ferrari finished with the aforementioned Canadian parachutist's arrival and reception at Bardi. As the last of the fugitives reached Bardi, a meeting took place at Chiesa Bianca, as had been agreed at Fontanellato by Ferrari and the head of the Allied delegation. The meeting had been arranged at the personal suggestion of our delegate, as explained above.[3]

The meeting at Chiesa Bianca in Bardi was held on 23 September, featuring a group of Allied officers and representatives of Parma's *Comitato d'azione antifascista* (Dante Gorreri, Giacomo Ferrari, Giovanni Molinari, Luigi Porcari and Ugo Nanni, in his capacity as interpreter). The intention was to agree on a common plan of action that would spur the formation of partisan units comprising Parma inhabitants, Allied soldiers and Yugoslavs. But no agreement was reached and the proposal foundered.[4]

However, several groups of former prisoners reached Bardi and were put up in the village for some time. As Giuseppe Lumia, a member of the local CLN, recalls, the first person to receive British soldiers was actually Francesco Berni, the prefectorial commissioner appointed by Parma's Fascist prefect.[5] At the end of the war he published in the provincial newspaper some letters received from Allied soldiers. "Signor Berni," write the officers Douglas, Elliot, Hudson, Badd, Thompson and Kenyon, "always did everything in his power to help the British prisoners of war and we hope that our government will always wish to help him in return if it proves necessary."[6] Another group of officers writes, "to make known the considerable assistance given us by Signor Berni from the middle of September 1943 onwards. This help was always given freely and without interruption."[7] Finally, F. A. Black, a RAF officer, writes how it was "hard for us English to be able to thank Signor Berni for all the help that he gave us during the year we were in these mountains. In his role as mayor [*sic*] of this town he supplied us with all the necessities of life."[8]

The participation of the Parma CLN was not confined to the initial period and to moving the Allied soldiers to the mountains; the connection remained active and useful subsequently, too. The collaboration between the local CLN and the British was always strong at Bardi, where escapers were constantly present, at least until the summer of 1944. During the 40 days when the village was the most important centre of the "free zone" (June and July 1944), "the Committee for Assistance to former British prisoners" was set up. It liaised closely with the democratic administration of the elected mayor, the lawyer Giuseppe Lumia. In an article written in 1945, Lumia recalls how "the administration, while taking proper steps to honour the fallen and bring comfort to those suffering, lost no time in improving the lot of the former British prisoners who had found refuge in Bardi. In order to help them cope with all kinds of shortages, at their request the ex-prisoners had ration cards and the means to get hold of goods instantly. I gave grants to all those who requested them during and after my term as mayor, and during and after the establishment of the Committee for Assistance to former British prisoners."[†]

[†] The ex-prisoners sheltered at Bardi, as recorded by Lumia, numbered about 40: Colonels Richards and de Bruyne; Major

The underground network set up in the hills and mountains also served to aid the former prisoners, as is clear from a document of the CLN of Fornovo Taro regarding "activity carried out on behalf of the Allied prisoners".[9] The initial contact with the local CLN was made by Lazzaro Bazzoni,‡ who lived at Mariano di Pellegrino Parmense. On 20 September, despite the German decree that threatened death to anybody who helped the prisoners, he let CLN comrades know that a number of former prisoners from Fontanellato had reached the mountains and that there was an urgent need for food and clothing. The first delivery of provisions followed five days later. The Fornovo CLN note records: "Bazzoni himself came to collect the things. Our activity continued in this way up to the middle of March 1944 and was notable not only for satisfying requirements for food but for meeting demands for other necessities."

An example of this was the attempt to recover personal effects left at Fontanellato. Guglielmo Tanzi recalls one such expedition:

> On 4 November I drove to the nuns at the *Santuario* at Fontanellato and to Signorina Testi to collect garments that the English officers Taylor, Holworthy and Ostle had left as they escaped...following that, on the 12th of the same

---

Fairley; Captains Badd and Black; Lieutenants Edwards, Rogers, Craddock, Blunt, Gee, Ballantyne, Rippondale, Taylor, Alexander and Goddard; Sergeant Flick; Privates J. Sutherland, N. Ross, T. Thompson, C. Verity, J. Sugdon, J. Sindcock, L. Canyon, L. Mason, F. Fields, R. Elliott, R. J. Starck, L. Jenkenson, Bernards, H. de Lisle, J. Hudson, H. Thompson, J. Murray, Rengon, T. Williams, S. Walts, A. Thompson, B. Crackle, T. Traynor. (G. Lumia [1945], *Bardi centrale di patriotteria*, Tipografia Fratelli Godi, pp. 32–33.) (It has been impossible in some cases to confirm that a name is spelt correctly.)

‡ Lazzaro Bazzoni and his wife were shot dead in "mysterious" circumstances in March 1945 near their home in Milan.

month I made a journey to Fontanellato to recover other objects belonging to the same Englishmen, but it was in vain because the Germans had removed absolutely everything belonging to the Englishmen.[10]

The Fornovo anti-Fascists continued to provide help throughout the winter. Luigi Sbodio, a member of the CLN of Fornovo, writes:

> It was clear that the assistance to the former Allied prisoners required all our goodwill in that it was a hard task to find money and groceries, especially in those early days, as the German death decree was still fresh in everybody's mind. However, we dealt with that and such actions went on until towards the end of March. During this period the following officers received assistance: Jack Younger, J. F. Taylor, R. G. Selby, [J. W.] Fairbrass, F. G. Cook, H. D. Holworthy, Ostle, N. S. Sonnger, W. Benzie, John W. Burman, John Baddeley, R. Brooke; and S. C. Page, a Private. And these Englishmen got fed on meat that mocked German arrogance: by agreement with the butcher Dallatomasina it was meat pilfered from the daily ration assigned to the German forces stationed at Fontanellato.[11]

Not all the British soldiers appeared fully to understand the risks run by their helpers, as is evident from Remo Polizzi's account of a journey he made to Bardi. This extract, one should note, refers to an episode that took place following the failure of the meeting at Chiesa Bianca, namely after the refusal of the Allied representatives to participate directly in the partisan struggle.

I remember that I once had to go to a family near Bardi where four or five of these former prisoners were lodging; they had asked to talk to someone in charge of the organisation. On arrival there to find out what they wanted, I heard myself being asked to take a couple of them back to Fontanellato, from where they had come, for a few days as they had to speak – so they said – to a woman they knew. In addition, they all complained that the food was monotonous and rather short of meat. I was left astonished by these demands, asking myself where they thought they were – in a village in wartime or on holiday! I replied as I had to, that I had no intention of risking either their lives or the lives of others.[12]

During the Christmas festivities the Fornovo committee received some thank-you letters from the British hiding at Mariano di Pellegrino. "To our Fornovo friends," writes Lt. Jack Younger in Italian, "I wish to thank you for all the things that you have sent to the English officers who are in the parish of Mariano for the Christmas festival. I must also thank you on my own behalf for all the help I have received in the past months. I am about to leave. I send you greetings and wish you good luck in the war against fascism and Nazism. I hope to find a way in which I can be of use to Italians fighting for a free Italy. Once again, a thousand thanks, and I end with the hope that I see you again soon, when the world is at peace. Long live Italy!"[13]

Lt. John Burman wanted to thank directly the people who had busied themselves in taking provisions to the Pellegrino hamlet during these months. "Dearest Signorine Davoli§: I am writing in English to thank you this time, because it is so much easier to express myself. We can't find

---

§ Ines Davoli ("Adriana") and Amelia Davoli ("Maria") were both members of the Fornovo Resistance.

the words to thank you for how much you have done and do for us. As you have my address, I would be very happy if you would like to write to me when this hullabaloo is over, so that I can also compensate you to some extent for your trouble. Our 'friend in common' tells me that perhaps it will be possible to see each other in the near future. I can't say other than that, at present, nothing would give me greater pleasure."[14]

The former prisoners and military representatives of the Resistance liaised with each other after the meeting at Chiesa Bianca as well. In some cases, although in truth these were few, Allied soldiers joined guerrilla bands. On 12 April, at Ponteceno d'Anzola (Bedonia), John Harrison (a trooper of the 7th Queen's Own Hussars) was killed during the first significant round-up carried out by German detachments in the Apennines of the Parma region. Harrison, Younger and "a number of other prisoners of war who had escaped from camps"[15] had joined the first of the partisan units on Mt. Penna. In an attempt to outflank the enemy, the two former prisoners and Count Carlo Cantelli, himself a partisan, ran into a military detachment in the neighbourhood of an inn in Ponteceno. They decided to attack it and hit several soldiers before retreating. Younger and "the Count"** managed to give the Germans the slip, but the wounded Harrison was captured and shot.[16] In another example of collaboration, on 4 December 1944 Anselmo Tanzi put the political commissioner of the 1st Julia Brigade in touch with officers staying at Mariano, with the aim of getting the Allies to do a parachute drop of arms and ammunition.

For the British still present in the Pellegrino area of Parma, the moment to depart came in March. In his book, Luigi Sbodio recalls that moment:

** Lt. Younger remained with the partisans of the 32nd Brigata Garibaldi "Monte Penna". In October 1944, he rejoined the 8th Army with a party of other escapers. Count Carlo Cantelli was killed during the winter round-ups in January 1945.

A breathless Bazzoni was with us, showing a sheet of paper obtained from a reliable source. The Republican police had got wind of "an English scent" near Mariano and the note was clear: "They will have to leave the place immediately." A decision was made. Some went to the Bardi area, others to Bedonia, and the rest (at their insistence) were directed to Milan for the journey to Switzerland. The Fidenza comrades, with whom Bazzoni was in touch, dealt with the latter. John Taylor, generally known to people who lived there as Giovanni "the tall", remained at Mariano because he was unwell.

The following evening Bazzoni – as agreed – was at Viazzano with two Englishmen: we sent a Lombatti company car to take them to the railway station. Once there, mixed up among us, we managed to get them onto the train under the noses of German and Fascist soldiers. Bazzoni accompanied them to their destination: the Bedonia area.[17]

The Mariano contingent was definitely only one of the groups of former prisoners who found refuge in the mountains and were in contact with the Resistance. Others gravitated to the higher Taro and Ceno valleys, while yet others avoided any contact whatsoever with partisans. However, despite the shortage of documents and precise evidence, there were certainly links between the anti-fascist movement and the Allied soldiers. One point of contact was the air-drops that the partisans received from the Allied forces, in which the former prisoners acted as intermediaries.

5. Freedom

For anyone looking for a way out, there were, as has been said, two possibilities: Switzerland or liberated Italy.* After the soldiers had left their refuge in the Bund (the Rovacchia stream) outside Fontanellato, some groups decided to set out directly for Switzerland or to join up with friendly troops. Other former prisoners, however, preferred to wait for a relaxation of the predictable wave of round-ups on the lowlands in search of those who had fled from the various camps. A number of testimonies survive to these two approaches that provide a fairly exact picture of what happened once the prisoners had crossed the orphanage's threshold.

Wing Commander Peter Bragg set off after one night in the Bund for Lake Como together with fellow RAF officers Derek Iles and Bill Rainford. Warned that the Germans would have heard a BBC broadcast stating that prisoners were targeting Como, they crossed the border east of Como and reached Campocologno in Switzerland on 22 September.[1] Captain Douglas Clarke, concerned by reports about the concentration of Germans and "fearing recapture", hid for some days in the Soragna area before setting off for the border. He arrived in Campocologno on 15 September thanks to help from guides.[2]

Not all the fugitives succeeded in establishing contacts, however. Lt. John R. Baynham and a companion decided to set off for Switzerland on foot, reaching the neighbourhood

---

* It is estimated from British intelligence sources that, in early October 1943, the number of prisoners who had escaped and about whom there was "no information as to their recapture" totalled approximately 26,500; 18,000 were in German hands, of whom 5,500 had already been taken to Germany; 2,175 had reached Allied lines; 1,200 were reported to be in Switzerland; and 25,500 were unaccounted for. National Archives, London, WO 224/179.

of Campocologno at midday on 26 September without having manged to link up with any organisation.[3]

There were also those, such as Lt. Col. Hugh Mainwaring's group, who chose to take an unusual route without delay in order to join up with friendly detachments. This was towards the Adriatic. The description that Mainwaring gave in his escape report, although in outline, is sufficiently clear.

> When the whole camp was dispersed Captain Camino offered to take Lt. Col. de Burgh, Lt. Col. Wheeler and Captain [Reggie] Phillips with him to his home in the Turin area, leaving me with Lt. [George] Lascaris (a Greek who had been serving at C.S.D.I.C. Middle East [Combined Services Detailed Interrogation Centre]) and Lt. [Leon] Blanchaert (a Belgian who had enlisted in the British forces in Egypt and had been doing a special job in the "Arab Legion").
>
> Lt. Lascaris, Lt. Blanchaert and I obtained civilian clothing from farms in the area. We had with us emergency rations – one tin of bully beef, one tin of meat roll and one tin of biscuits among the three of us. We then proceeded to walk south to join the 8th Army in the Foggia area. Our route was: S. E. across the Via Emilia to south of Parma – along the Via Emilia and about ten miles south of it to beyond Bologna – across to the north of the Via Emilia direct to the coast to Cesenatico – along the coast approximately 25 miles inland to Casa Calendra [Casacalenda] where we passed through the German line and made contact with the K.O.Y.L.I. [King's Own Yorkshire Light Infantry] at 0900 hours, 13 October.
>
> We had walked all the time except for 36 hours at Cesenatico, where we were trying to get a boat. Except at Cesenatico we never disclosed that we

were British P/W, but came all the way as returning Italian soldiers. We were faced with the danger of capture by the Germans and of apprehension by the Italian authorities. The Germans had offered an award of 2,600 lire (or £20) for the notification of the whereabouts of any British P/W. We therefore decided that, as far as possible, we must not disclose our British identity.

Lt. Lascaris is a fluent Italian speaker. Lt. Blanchaert is a good Italian speaker. I am a bad Italian speaker and anything I said would at once disclose my identity and probably that of the others. We therefore decided to pose throughout the journey as Italian soldiers endeavouring to return to their homes in southern Italy.

The story we used was always the same, but as we moved towards the coast our point of origin had to be changed. The story in the later stages was as follows. We were three Italian soldiers (myself in the Labour Corps) who had been conscripted and absent from home for four years. When the Armistice was declared we were in Zagreb (Yugoslavia). We got on a train and went to Trieste, where the train was searched by the Germans for Italian personnel. Shooting took place and we among others were taken P/W with a view to our removal to Germany. This had been too much for me, and I had had a nervous breakdown, the symptoms of which were complete silence except for muttering a few words about my family to my friends: I would not talk to strangers. After two days' captivity in Trieste, we had managed to escape and had decided to do the remainder of the journey on foot […]

Passing thus as Italians, we had no difficulty in obtaining the food and shelter which the Italian peasant was prepared to give to his own kind in the circumstances outlined in our story. The food consisted of bread, an occasional egg, a small piece of cheese, and permission to take fruit and tomatoes growing in the fields. When we asked for it we were given shelter at night time in outhouses, barns, cattle sheds, etc.[4]

Captain Carol Mather, unlike Mainwaring, chose to attempt the high passes in his quest to meet up with the Allies. Together with Lt. Archie Hubbard, he travelled along the Apennines: Berceto, Castelnuovo Monti, Pavullo, Marradi, Mercato, Pennabilli, Cagli, San Severino, Gran Sasso – right up to Casacalenda, where they came across men of the 5th Division, Eighth Army. The journey took 38 days, during which the two soldiers, dressed in civilian clothes, constantly received help from the population in the form of food, lodging and, sometimes, money.[5]

Captain Michael Gilbert, accompanied by Lt. Tony Davies, also headed south along the Apennine ridge. In his escape report he recalls: "We avoided places altogether and made contact with practically no civilians. On 25 October I lost Lt. Davies when we were fired at by a German sentry and had to run for it, just south of Castel di Sangro. I have not seen him again." Gilbert met up with friendly troops near Lucito,[6] while Davies was wounded and captured by German units.[7]

Luigi Leoni, a member of the Resistance at Rusino, in the municipality of Tizzano Val Parma, remembers that former prisoners were continually passing by.

The English prisoners used to go towards Pavullo in the Modena region, then carry on and get through the Front Lines. Rusino was one of the early stages on their journey. A group of three or four men, usually including one who spoke Italian, used to come every week; they would refuel, have a wash and then leave. They continued to come past until late autumn.

This was the procedure: get everybody involved, the whole population. There was this proclamation that said that if you help a prisoner you are doomed. So we sent the prisoners to everybody, even to a Fascist's. He didn't object and so from that moment onwards he was involved and he too had to keep quiet.

Parma's underground movement organised everything. The English were of course polite, gentlemanly and not obsequious. I remember one whose father had a villa at Rapallo and, among others, a group of quite elderly officers, who were bank managers. They used to want to pay for the soup, if they possibly could, but we never wanted anything.[8]

Under the false impression that there would be an Allied landing in Liguria, several groups, such as the four soldiers led by Captain Peter Barshall, set off in a south-westerly direction, in a short time reaching Monte Desio, a few kilometres from Pieve Cusignano. They hoped to cross the Apennines and get to La Spezia, where it was thought that a disembarkation of friendly troops was most likely. The four men, persuaded by the *contadini* not to risk the move there, remained the guests of families in the area: *casa* Tripoli (Pietro and Emilio Casselli) and *casa* Giorgina (Arno Fontanesi, Nino Fontana and Dante Demo). When the absence of an Allied landing made a journey to Liguria futile, the four looked for useful contacts to get them across enemy lines. But the difficulty in singling out credible intermediaries and, above all, their hosts' growing anxiety (several Fascist patrols had been spotted in the area) persuaded the former prisoners to attempt a journey north.

By means of a "private organisation" and with the help of some Milan friends of Barshall, the quartet first got to Milan, then Como and then to the Swiss border. It is interesting to note the means and the route by which they reached the frontier: by taxi from Pieve Cusignano to Fidenza, where a railwayman got train tickets for Milan. The journey was interrupted four times by stops for searches, all of which they got through. In Milan the British spent the night in an air-raid shelter, dodging the police patrols checking identity cards. The following morning, still by train, they went to Como, where they had an appointment with a guide who accompanied them in a taxi along the eastern shore of the lake. At Nesso they were joined by two smugglers who rowed them as far as Brienno, where they went up into the mountains in a westerly direction, crossing the border north-east of Cabbio.[9]

The case of Lt. John de Bendern and Captain A. P. Mitchell appears from the records to be unusual. They chose to return to Montalbo, where they had been incarcerated prior to Fontanellato, in the hope of obtaining assistance from "some friendly Italians" they knew there. But "there were too many Germans" at Montalbo and, after finding refuge 10 kilometres away, the search of a neighbouring house persuaded them to leave the Piacenza region and attempt the crossing over to Switzerland. This was successful with the help "of a smuggler".[10]

Apart from those who left immediately for the Swiss border or went south, any escapers who stayed put for a time depended on the fellowship of the Parma *contadini*. One ex-prisoner estimated that in the immediate aftermath of the escape approximately 200 former prisoners found temporary refuge in homes on the plain.[11]

Although all-in-all the Swiss route appeared the shortest and quickest, it was fraught with difficulties. It was all but impossible to cross north Italy without any help, closely monitored as it was by German and Fascist troops, to say nothing of the natural barriers between it and Switzerland.

On the other hand, for anyone deciding to stay put it was exceedingly difficult to gauge how the population would react in the face of repeated requests for food, clothing and lodging. Unknown and, one imagined, hostile territory made both choices highly dangerous. It was certainly easier to hide in the high Apennine valleys to avoid the German raids and the possibility that Fascists would inform on them.

Lt. Mike Goldingham's sketch of a contadino *offering refuge in a barn*

Those hiding near Fontanellato in the homes of the *contadini* spent varying lengths of time there. Undecided or resigned, they waited before undertaking a journey towards unknown mountains or across a plain thick with the enemy and with a population that one might imagine to be unfriendly. Captain Noel H. Burdett and Major G. H. D. Collins, for example, stayed in the area as guests of the Panciroli family at Cannetolo di Fontanellato from 11 September to 6 October. After evading capture many times (there were frequent raids hunting for the PG 49 prisoners) they chose to move to Parma. They passed through Fontanellato one last time, where Ferruccio Incerti kitted them out with clothes and took them to Parma. They found shelter there until 21 November with the family of

Ferdinando Incerti, their escort's relation, whose house was in Strada dell'Università. For seven weeks the two men busied themselves in trying to track down a contact who could make a discreet expatriation possible. According to Burdett's testimony, the pair were betrayed but managed to escape recapture by hiding on the roof during a Fascist raid. Through "friends" they made contact with members of the *Italia Libera*[†] organisation, which arranged travel for them to Milan and thence over the border. Burdett also reported that during their stay at Parma both he and Collins had been assisted by the Sergiacomi family (who lived in Via Fabio Filzi, 11) and by a certain Signora Bianchi. Eventually, the two men crossed the frontier during the night of 3 December near the village of Casalino, north-east of Como.[12]

Captain J. G. Canning and Captain A. J. Green made a similar choice to that of Burdett and Collins. After leaving the Bund they "wandered about the Plain of Lombardy for a few days seeking definite information on which to base plans for rejoining [the] Allies".[13] They remained hidden for two months at the home of a *contadino*, Paolo Rossetti, at Corticelli di San Secondo, with the collaboration of other *contadini* in the zone who provided hospitality, clothing, food and money. Gino Cantoni, in the hamlet of Grugno, Ernesto Rastelli and the Frazzi family, of Corticelli, were among the most active. According to Canning's escape report, Rossetti "acted as interpreter for the Germans and was in a position to supply us with information of any German suspicions regarding the harbouring of any PoWs in that area".

The two Englishmen chose to stay on the plain and await events, considering it too risky to go up into the mountains and aim for Allied lines. Subsequently, on learning that it was possible to get back to Britain from Switzerland, they

---

[†] *Italia Libera* took its name from the title of the newspaper of the *Partito d'Azione*.

decided to make the attempt. From Castelguelfo they went by train as far as Luino.[14]

Canning goes on:

> We left with a young woman known to us as Dulcina who was acting as a guide. We arrived at Luino on the same day (7.12.1943) and the three of us walked as far as Valdomino, where Dulcina was to put us in touch with a *passeur*. He would have nothing to do with us, however, as the parish priest and two hundred villagers had been arrested and removed by the Germans that morning. As it was then late I suggested to Green that we leave Valdomino and seek safety in the woods until morning when we could seek a *passeur*. Some distance on we came to a small cottage in which a woman and a girl were working. In the course of conversation I became convinced that they were anti-fascist and I felt able to entrust them with our plans. It transpired that their brother, one Bertoli, was a *passeur* who was helping an Italian Jew to cross to Switzerland on the following night and we were told that if we wished we could join the party. We accepted and paid Bertoli 2,000 lire for his services. We left at 2100 hours on 8 December and entered Switzerland at Termine Tessin at 0600 hours on 9 December.[15]

To get to Switzerland one had to confront obstacles that could not always be overcome without help: the language, the presence of Germans and Fascists, and the need for civilian clothes, food and shelter at night. The aid of a guide was useful if the enterprise were to come off, and practically indispensable when it came to completing the last stage. This assistance could be found without charge through one of the many political organisations sympathetic to the Allies, or for a fee through the private ones that had sprung up in those weeks in response to requests from the thousands of Allied fugitives anxious to reach the Swiss frontier. But these requests were not from former prisoners alone: Jewish citizens, disbanded Italian soldiers and anti-Fascists on the run all sought to avoid capture by the Germans. Lt. Richard N. Brooke recalls: "Various private organisations were heard of which appeared to operate with varying success, most of which charged large sums for taking PoWs to Switzerland. The best appeared to be the *Partito d'Azione*, which was thoroughly well organised."[16]

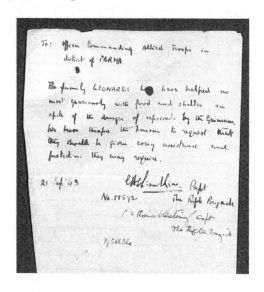

A note left by Captain Anthony Simkins and Captain Philip Morris-Keating with the Leonardi family of Borgo Val di Taro, thanking them for sheltering them after their escape from PG 49

Convinced that it was better to await events before taking a decision, a large number of prisoners opted for the mountains, awaiting the moment to attempt to flee the country. Others, once up in the mountains, tried to reach Allied lines by travelling along the Apennine ridge as others who had left earlier had done. For example, Captain Eric S. Cutler and three fellow soldiers left the Bund and wandered around the Parma countryside before electing to take the high route. They stayed with Professor Pietro Negri Avanzini, who lived at Cannetolo di Fontanellato, and then for about a month with Andrea Baruffini's family. From there they moved to Medesano, near Parma, where they found bed and board with the Grandi, Fossi, Foglia and Albertini families, and after that with Silvio Bonati at Noceto.

Returning to the plain, the four men went to Parma where they looked for an organisation to help them make the final leap towards freedom. They received help from the following families during their stay in the town: Bertoli, at Via M. D'Azeglio, 24; Azzali, at Via Dalmazia, 23; and Meli. Thanks to the good offices of Gianni Granuello, of Castelguelfo, who got hold of food, money and cigarettes for the journey north, they went by train to Milan where they stayed for three weeks, assisted by a group of students (Angelo Mainardi, Luigi Turconi and Giuseppe Fenocchi, who himself came from Medesano). They belonged to an organisation, possibly *Italia Libera*, commanded by an engineer whose name the men never knew. It was the "Davis" organisation that proved to be the key to getting the four men out of Italian territory, by the proven route of Intragna, Avrano, Socraggio, Cavaglio and Brissago, where they arrived on 1 March 1944. Based at Intragna, above Intra, the organisation was led by Lt. "Arca", who, according to information from Cutler, succeeded in conveying about 250 former Allied prisoners to Switzerland.[17]

Captain Reginald Benson, instead, went directly to Bardi. "I stayed for two weeks owing to bad feet. After the snow arrived I moved into a house in the River Arda area where I stayed until approx. 9 December 1943, when an organisation contacted me and I left on foot for Piacenza, and then by train for Milan, staying with the guide there for five days. We left by train for the north, then walked for 16 hours finally arriving at the frontier of Switzerland on 16 December 1943, assisted in the last move by smugglers."[18]

Lt. Richard N. Brooke and Lt. Jack Younger went on 12 September to Mariano di Pellegrino Parmense, a place which, like Banzola and Bardi, was welcoming to the former prisoners. They stayed for several months with the families of Ida Papisca and Lazzaro Bazzoni, who gave them clothes, food and lodging. During their stay they got in touch with people in the Resistance in the Bedonia area and joined a partisan unit. At the end of one action, disappointed by the "poor organisational level" of the band (the armed struggle was still in its infancy), the two soldiers abandoned the group and returned to Pellegrino Parmense. Younger, as is mentioned earlier, eventually crossed to Allied lines to reach safety but Brooke set out for Switzerland, arriving on 24 April 1944. According to his debriefing report, with the assistance of a guide made available by *Partito d'Azione*, Brooke travelled "by train Fidenza–Milan–Varese and thence in a train to a small village only a mile from the frontier. Then by foot to the wire, under the wire, where a small drain ran underneath it – across a river and thence to Pontetresa. A very easy, practical route."[19]

Lt. John Burman and Lt. William Benzie also went to the area of Mariano di Pellegrino. They spent some months as guests of numerous families in the Stirone valley, moving between Pellegrino, Salsomaggiore, Varano Marchesi and Vernasca (Piacenza). They then managed to get in touch with people they believed to be partisans but who "we discovered to be mostly of the 'bandit' type. We had nothing further to do with these people."[20] After returning to Mariano with the help of an "organisation", they went to Milan, Lake Maggiore and then into Switzerland. Burman remembers the final stage of the journey, in particular:

> [A] guide arrived at [the] house of Lazzaro Bazzoni to take Captain J. Moore, Lt. P. Bruen and two other officers to Switzerland. As these

four had gone back to the mountains for a short period and were therefore unavailable Lt. Benzie and myself were invited to go in their places. We were taken by car to Fidenza, by rail to Milan and from Milan to Lovena [Laveno] on Lake Maggiore. We crossed to Intra and walked to Brissago with guides…There were two male and one female guide.[21]

In Benzie's version they were handed over to partisans at Intra. One of these, he says, was Bazzoni, who lived at Casa Masaschi at Mariano di Pellegrino. Bazzoni "did excellent work and was a tireless worker on behalf of British escaped PoWs".[22]

Iside Fontana and her father, Nino, c. 1949

Captain Harold C. Carver spent a short time on the plain with a *contadino* family. Alerted that "we had been given away", he switched to the mountains around Banzola (Salsomaggiore), where he stayed for about ten days, "going from house to house", until he met another former prisoner who took him to the home of Albino Albertini at Medesano. There he stayed for one month. After every attempt to contact an organisation had failed, Carver decided to move to Parma, where he hoped to have better luck. He stayed there until the end of January, lodging at the home of Nando Ferri, at Borgo Lalatta, 6. He was also supported by the Meli family, who lived in the same building, and by the Fontana family, who provided food, in particular. Carver spent the last fortnight in a woodshed, still in the town, before leaving with Captain John Greenwood for Lake Maggiore, escorted by the Italian captain from PG 49, Jack Camino. The pair crossed the border on 8 February and the mountain guide "neither asked for nor received any money from us".[23]

Iside Fontana lived with her parents at Noceto. When prisoners fleeing from Fontanellato began to arrive in search of assistance, she was 14 years old. It was, above all, the memory of four British officers who stayed around her home for some time that impressed itself on the young woman.

> They came up here. My Dad [Nino] was not a Fascist and we felt we should help them. They didn't arrive on their own. Someone directed them, accompanied them. The neighbours did not know they were here. My Dad also had contacts who would have helped them reach Switzerland. There were so many who passed this way. They thought they would find a hiding place, given that it was a little out in the wild here. Besides, my Mum also took in many Italian soldiers who had run away from their barracks. We took some of these English to my aunt's at Montesalso above Varano Melegari, and those that couldn't be sorted out found a refuge on Mt. Desio. They dug out a cave and hid there. Some didn't know a word of Italian, like that 40-year-old Scottish

major. I remember he didn't know how to ride a bicycle that my sister brought from my aunt's. Then there was a round-up and I don't know what happened to him. However, when there was a raid or some action they used to go up to their den on the mountain [...]

About 30 will have passed by us but I can say I knew only four of them well: a colonel whom they called Pop, meaning Dad, Major James, Lt. John and Captain Peter Barshall. They made a big impression on me. In the eyes of a country girl, they were so educated and distinguished, among us country people, that I was really struck, right from the start – to such an extent that I fell in love with the idea of going to see where they lived. I remember when Pop, who spoke Italian quite well, related to me one evening when he came to our house for the night, how he had learned of the death of his son, who was killed during the Sicily landings while he himself was at Fontanellato. He had dignity, he was educated, a big, good-looking man, tall and distinguished. He said that they had been all right at Fontanellato. He still had in his kitbag the remains of the last parcel received before leaving the camp. He gave much of the food to my Mum [...]

When Italy was liberated there was nobody left. In one way or another, they had all gone away. My Dad and [Arno] Fontanesi escorted several of them towards Switzerland. Arriving at a certain point they handed them over to other people. When the war ended I wanted to go to England. My Dad had the address of the firm in Milan where Captain Barshall had gone back to work. I had a cousin who was studying at Milan university. We got hold of Barshall through him. I told him in a letter that I wished to go to

England and could they put me up in a college in order to learn English. It wasn't easy to ask him this but I did it. He replied immediately and organised everything. So I went to London, to his office in the City, a terrifying affair. I had never seen anything like it. He was very well-to-do. He had sent me the tickets he had paid for himself, and the address of the family who would put me up; they were his friends. The family was that of the headteacher of the school I attended; it was in Kent. I felt myself at a disadvantage not being able to speak so the headteacher asked some of his pupils to teach me a little. But I was too much of a country girl and wasn't yet 19.

I stayed for a year at the college, a convent school founded in 1909 – all paid for by the Barshall family. I spent Christmas with the family [at the college] and also went to see Peter Barshall's family at his firm's offices. I remember that Peter's father summoned all the employees to show them the girl who had looked after his son [...]

A few days before returning home, I was at the college and the doorbell rings. The nun can't open the door so she asks me to do it as the engineer had arrived. I went and opened the door. This man was there...it was as if I had been hit by a bolt of lightning, it was my destiny, just like in a fairy tale. We exchanged a few words and, [discovering] it was my birthday, he said: "We must celebrate! Come at seven and have tea at my house." All his family was there. When I arrived he introduced me to everybody and showed me around the house, we had tea and it ended with us seeing each other twice more. But I had to go back home and I was not at all pleased...However, we then wrote to each other and after three months he came to Italy and we got married in August. Back in England, Robert and I were together for 42 years.[24]

Another informative report comes from Captain Charles Castle. After staying, along with Captain K. Frazer, around Fontanellato and Fidenza for about a week, Castle set off south, reaching the Taro river beyond Bardi. He "investigated stories of rebel formations", and unsuccessfully tried to work out a way to join the Allies. He went back to the Fidenza district on foot, considering it too dangerous in the mountains as several British officers and Other Ranks had been arrested by the Fascists and the Germans.

Castle continues:

> Louis Bertorelli, who had previously assisted us, endeavoured to find a way to get us to Switzerland but was unable to get in touch with any organisation. He took us himself by train to Milan and kept us hidden for three days while trying to find us a guide to take us on. Captain Frazer then went on to Ponte Chiasso and reconnoitred possibilities of crossing the frontier. He sent me a message back the same evening that he had found a possible route.
>
> I went to Como the same evening, 23 December 1943, and managed to purchase the return half of a bus ticket to Ponte Chiasso from an Italian. I proceeded there and contacted Captain Frazer who informed me that he had found a place just outside the village where the frontier wire had been broken down by a landslide. We decided to jump and run for it immediately as it was just before the 2200 hours curfew. We proceeded along the road and on reaching the place jumped and ran. There were

two German sentries, one Italian sentry and watch dogs at the spot. The Germans fired on us and Captain Frazer was recaptured (I believe unwounded). I ran on, forded the river and was met by a Swiss frontier guard who took me to Chiasso.[25]

Lt. John G. Dean also retraced his steps, having stayed with the manager of the inn at Banzola (Attilio Oppici) and at Varano Melegari (Daniele Castelli). He reached Fidenza, where he stayed nearly four weeks with the Volanti family. He got to the Swiss border near Como at the end of December with the help of a "guide", Rinaldo Galli from Fidenza, who handed him over "to another guide at the lake side". The guide "was not really part of an organisation, but acted on his own".[26]

Captain Robert Williams, in company with a fellow Indian Army officer (Captain T. G. Philipsz), went into the mountains and spent four months between Bardi and the villages of the Taro valley, before moving off towards Tuscany where they hoped to find a more "Royalist" and less "Red" population than that of the Parma region appeared to be.[27]

Williams wrote in his diary at the end of September 1943: "These Italians have shaken us; we thought nowt of them before (I still can't say I respect them at all), but their generosity has shown us how a bad government can ruin a happy people. *'Povera Italia'*, as they all say, often with tears in their eyes [behaviour that in another passage he calls 'boring' and 'whining']. After a dinner of bread and milk (our choice), they actually came to put us to bed in the straw, bless them again! And to think that three weeks ago we were their enemies!"[28]

127

6. The Victims

Many attempts to regain freedom were unsuccessful and, inevitably, the capture of a fugitive ended in involving civilians who had come to his aid. This letter to a Fascist at Fontanellato on 31 October 1943 was written by Captain C. D. Patterson: "When you captured my friends at 9 p.m. on 28 October, I was lucky to get away. I am writing to tell you that I shall never forget and that one day we shall be able to meet again in more favourable circumstances for me and my friends. You played a nasty trick not only on us but also on your fellow citizens. I can understand that someone might wish to capture English evaders, but not betray one's own fellow countrymen in the way that you did."[1]

In several instances, names were found on papers discovered in captured prisoners' possession; sometimes these were diaries kept by those prisoners. The consequences were always disastrous.

The case of the Cervi family, from Gattatico, between Parma and Reggio Emilia, stands out among the many cases cited within the records of the Allied Screening Commission, which was appointed to identify and reimburse civilians who had assisted escapers. Among the *contadini* of the Emilia region, theirs was the most famous example of sacrifice for the anti-fascist cause. It is referred to in the Commission's papers as a case of "courageous generosity" towards the Allied ex-prisoners on the run.[2]

The anonymous author of "Report on the Cervi family of Gattatico" for the Commission states:

> The case of the Cervi family is one of the most tragic cases to have come to the notice of this Commission. The seven sons (three were married) were all shot on 28 December 1943. The elder sons had always been anti-Fascist and communist; the eldest had served a term of

imprisonment in 1939 and again in 1942 for political reasons.

In November 1943 all the brothers with their families lived together in the family home with their father [Alcide] and mother. At this time the partisan bands were not well organised. The younger brothers acted as guides taking PoWs to safe hide-outs in the mountains, and being a very prosperous *contadino* family, they were able to provide food and clothing to many of the large number of PoWs who were in the area.

On 25 November 1943 the house was surrounded by Fascists who had been informed the PoWs were hidden there. The search produced five PoWs: two British, a South African, a Frenchman and a Russian. The father and his seven sons were arrested, taken to the prison at Servi (Reggio Emilia), after five days in San Tommaso prison.

Some time before 28 December 1943, the Secretary of the Prefect was shot by a member of the underground movement; as a reprisal for this the seven brothers were themselves shot on 28 December. The father escaped from the prison, the wall of his cell having been destroyed in a bombing raid, and returned home. For months he remained hidden.

His wife died of grief in November 1944 and he attended the funeral, making his first appearance in the open. He was seen by the Germans who pardoned him and he was given his freedom.

At Fontanellato itself there were a number of people who paid with prison terms for extending hospitality to the men of PG 49, some of whom have already been mentioned. Andrea Baruffini, however, who was arrested and deported to the concentration camp at Mauthausen, in Austria, from where he did not return, was one who paid with his life.

Even in documented form, the events involving Baruffini and Lt. Gordon H. Beazley, who was one of the soldiers who had stayed at the family's house near the Bund (the Rovacchia stream) following the escape from the camp, have a dramatic air.

The Cervi family

The route taken by Beazley and the strategies that he adopted to avoid capture throw light on the steps taken by the men of PG 49 as they roamed around the province after 9 September. For Beazley, however, these came to an end on the evening of 31 January 1944 with his arrest at Parma.

Some notebooks were found in his room, in the form of a diary. Names, addresses, comments and events during his period of freedom were all recorded. There is no longer any trace of the notebooks, which fell into the hands of the Fascist police, but a long report that Alberto Bettini, the Parma police commissioner, sent to the then-chief of the province, Antonio Valli, survives. Substantial passages from the seized diary were reproduced in it.

In the first place, one learns from the report that Beazley, having got away from Fontanellato, had "wandered from village to village...mixing among the mass of country people, naturally giving the towns a wide berth, and questioning men and women, old and young, in order to find out about German and Italian troop movements". All this was done while observing orders given before leaving the Bund "to be wary and low-key, and to eke out our rations for as long as possible".[3] The important part played "by the women of the village" emerges yet again from his diary. According to the commissioner, "they competed with each other in taking food and clothing to them [the former prisoners]".

What alarmed Bettini was that Beazley knew all the main facts concerning the movement of German and Allied troops during that time. He knew "even the names of German generals going from one front or another to make inspections". Probably exaggerating, he places Beazley "at the centre of non-stop and intensive espionage, so much so that he often finds himself face-to face with a great many other individuals, probably English military spies, who come and go from one village to another in north Italy". These were in addition to "local people, whose names he shrewdly does not give, confining himself just to the initial of a baptismal name".

However, a number of names of people with whom Beazley had been in contact do appear in the first of the notebooks quoted. Without citing them in full, the commissioner gives their nationalities: Dalmatian-Croats, Montenegrins (probably escapers from the camp at Scipione (Salsomaggiore)), English, Americans, Australians and Argentinians. Several Italian names crop up in the same pages, corresponding largely to those who had busied themselves in helping him: Andrea Baruffini and Alice Belmori of Cannetolo, Volumnia Ugolotti, Alberto Guerino and Doctor Ravazzoni (at Via Collegio Maria Luigia in

Parma), Maria Oppici of Pieve di Cusignano, Paride Tonella and Lino Maiardi.

It is clear from Bettini's reconstruction that the assistance provided by the *contadini* was not always free of charge. This is confirmed by documentation tracked down at the archive of Parma's Historical Institute comprising acknowledgments and receipts for services rendered to the escaped prisoners.

Beazley's stay at the Baruffini family's home, and that of his companions, lasted until the first week of October. A meeting to plan the move to the mountains had taken place on Sunday 26 September. Bettini writes in his report: "He [Beazley] went to Baruffini's where he met [Silvio] Bonati, from Noceto, an employee at the Banca Commerciale in Parma, who gave him a sum of money and other addresses [...] of people at Banzola." Bonati, writes Beazley, "is a really good man who promised to come to see us often". Bonati hands him "a 1,000-lira note and then a further 3,000 lire". Remo Gandini, who supplied new civilian clothes, was present on that occasion.

Beazley's group left for the mountains on 5 October and reached "a wood from where they enjoyed a delightful view, almost as good as in Scotland, from a castle owned by an Englishman in Tabiano. That night they climbed a hill, in disguise: nobody realised anything." The text quotes Beazley directly: "After a rest we listened to the radio in several languages [...], Silvio arrived later; he had met up with Dr. R. [Ravazzoni], who was very pleased and was looking for me. He remembered my name, my regiment and my age." Dr. Giuseppe Ravazzoni had first met Beazley when the latter was being treated at Parma infirmary during his imprisonment at PG 49. That evening the special message they had been waiting for came through on the radio at last: "Tevere, Tevere" and "Simonetta has arrived". The group was ready to go down to the plain.

However, the stay in the mountains was extended until 26 October. In the meantime, the four-strong group made a number of contacts, including with disbanded Italian soldiers who had arrived at Medesano and who "bring news that the Germans had seized as hostages the parents of soldiers dodging the draft". They also met "local rebels" who said "Good Morning". There were others, too, "especially soldiers on the run, so-called rebels", among whom were three Parma students who "promised to bring us books in English".

Beazley reached Parma on the morning of 26 October: "I went into Carmen's house, next to the station; Carmen went to the bank, saying that Silvio would come at 12.30, and in fact he did. They went together to the doctor's house, but he was not there."

Beazley remained at Parma as a guest for some days. On the afternoon of 18 November there was an incident that seemed to add urgency to the situation. "The landlord came back with news that a priest had been shot at Torricella for having sheltered a (British) prisoner of war. We decided to leave; in a hurry to have another meeting with Dr. R. we went to the bank. After a short wait, Dr. R. arrived and greeted me warmly. Then we had a long talk. His family was away, his apartment was empty except for some old furniture and a radio."

Beazley remained the guest of Volumnia Ugolotti, a nurse who worked with Dr. Ravazzoni, until his capture on 31 January 1944.* He was together with a second British prisoner, whom we know only by his first name, Eric. (This is likely to be Captain Eric S. Cutler.)

---

* After interrogation Lt. Beazley was taken to a PoW camp in Moosberg and thence to Oflag VII-B at Eichstätt, Bavaria. He was liberated by the Americans in 1945 after hiding in the roof of a hut as the Germans evacuated the camp. In his military intelligence report he said that Andrea Baruffini had taken charge of the PG 49 documents and hidden them in his house, together with a letter from Captain E. S. Cutler to be delivered to the Area Commander after the occupation by British troops. National Archives WO 342/22/2; Beazley family records.

If, at first, Beazley's journey down to Parma seems to suggest an imminent attempt to reach the Swiss border – confirmed by the contacts and notes he made during a second brief stay in the Parma Apennines in early November – it appears in fact that "Beazley is more of an intelligence officer than a simple absconder".

Reporting on Beazley's writings, the Parma police commissioner refers to numerous meetings that the Englishman held with members of the Parma underground, never mentioned by name, and to several conversations with his interlocutors, in particular Dr. Ravazzoni. The doctor comes over as a dyed-in-the-wool anti-German and decisively on the side of the Allies. Beazley writes: "It is unbelievable how greatly I was liked by the family, in particular the children. The doctor's way of talking about the defeat of the Germans was especially surprising, and that was in the presence of the women of the house."

And again: "In this house bottles are at the ready to celebrate news that Rome has been taken; everybody here is in favour of the complete annihilation of the Germans." The portrait of the doctor that emerges from the English lieutenant's words is undoubtedly that of a confirmed supporter of Marshal Badoglio.[4]

The affair had a tragic epilogue, both for the Parma host and the Fontanellato host. The Parma police commissioner gave a precise description in a letter that he sent to the chief of police, Tullio Tamburini, on 19 February 1944.† Andrea Baruffini was picked up at his home at Cannetolo di Fontanellato on 11 March 1944, as his sons, Fortunato and Sandro, record:

> After the publication of the proclamation [against hosting prisoners of war], my father sent them [the former PoWs] to some friends of his in the mountains, in the direction of Banzola where he

---

† See Appendix 3.

was very well known…He continued to send them food: two or three times a week my sister used to set off on a bicycle…Then towards November they came back and again stayed at our house for a short time…Then, proclamations, spies, local Fascists…they seized him at home, at Cannetolo, Fascist militia surrounded the house and…He had been in the war of '11–'12 [the Italo-Turkish war over Libya], he had fought in the war of '15–'18 when he was promoted to marshal on the battlefield, and he had acted as a humanitarian…It is clear that he annoyed somebody, the Fascists. He was locked up in San Francesco prison in Parma. Something happened there…the prison was bombed and he could have escaped but he thought, "if I run away, they will take my children", they had already done that with his daughter, and he thought that might be done again. So he didn't dare flee.

From Parma, Baruffini was taken to Fossoli and from there to Bolzano, eventually reaching Mauthausen concentration camp on 5 July 1944. He died on 11 April 1945. "We knew nothing, we didn't know where he was. He had left us a final message written on a little piece of paper left behind at Fossoli. He wrote: 'Pray for me, destination unknown.' We heard nothing more of him."[5]

Appendix 1

This is an edited version of a report in the National Archives,* London, on the visit to the prison camp at Fontanellato on 14 May 1943 by officials of the Swiss Legation, which represented British interests in Italy.

After the inspection, Captain Leonardo Trippi, head of the Swiss delegation, compiled a long report based on several meetings he had held with Lt. Col. Eugenio Vicedomini, the Italian Commandant, Lt. Col. D. S. Norman, the prisoners' Senior Officer, and the prisoners themselves. In his findings, Trippi gave a comprehensive account of the camp, dwelling in particular on its capacity, the living conditions and whether the prisoners had complaints.

REPORT ON PRISONER OF WAR CAMP No. 49
Visited on 14 May 1943

Camp Commandant: Lt. Col. Eugenio Vicedomini
Camp Leader: Lt. Col. Norman
Capacity of camp: 500 Officers; 120 Orderlies

1. General

The officers who were formerly interned in Camp no. 41 and Camp no. 17 have been transferred to this new Camp no. 49. The majority of the detained are British officers – captains, lieutenants and second lieutenants. There are a few American officers and an American war correspondent.

Complying with the request of Lt. Col. Sam Agee, of the US army, we asked the War Ministry to transfer the American internees to a camp for American officers.

The camp is located on a plain about 197 feet above sea level, close to an agricultural centre. It is surrounded by fields and vine plantations; the climate is healthy. There are no

---

* National Archives, London; Foreign Office, 916/652.

industrial districts and cities in the neighbourhood, and it can be said that the camp is not in a danger zone.

The camp covers a total area of 210,000 square feet; 92,000 square feet are covered with structures, the rest is open and can be used as sports grounds.

The internees are quartered in a four-storeyed house, solidly built of stone and bricks at the beginning of the war and intended to be an orphanage. The beautiful building, with up-to-date installations, has not yet been used for its original purpose.

The vast premises allow the camp to be organised suitably. There are mess-rooms for both officers and orderlies, reading rooms, a bar, a library, a high and vast hall, offices, stores for various purposes and workshops. The quarters leave nothing to be desired.

2. The Camp

The offices, mess-rooms and showers are located on the ground floor. The first floor is occupied by officers' dormitories, a large hall, a bar, a recreation room, two toilet-rooms and water closets and a barber's shop. The other two floors are also appropriated for bedrooms for the officers; the toilet arrangements and WCs are identical to those on the first floor. The accommodation for the orderlies is on the top floor.

The roomy dormitories are high and airy; large windows let in plenty of sun and air and overlook the fertile plain. In every room there are two to four electric lamps and radiators for central heating. The officers have light, varnished iron beds with elastic springs, mattresses of wool, horsehair or artificial fibre, bedlinen and two blankets.

The interior arrangements are comfortable. There are separate night-tables for each bed, a fairly large wardrobe for every two officers, tables and chairs. There is a dormitory holding 30 beds and other, smaller, dormitories on each floor. The Camp Leader has a large room to himself.

A group of PoWs believed to have been photographed at PG 49, possibly during the inspection carried out by the Swiss Legation, 14 May 1943. Lt. Thomas Harris-Matthews and Lt. Frank Adams are standing third and fourth from the left. Other prisoners are unidentified

The men [Other Ranks] sleep in double-tier wooden beds provided with a mattress and two blankets; no bedlinen is provided for them. A dormitory, measuring 20 by 82 feet and 13 feet high, accommodates 53 men; there is a distance of about three feet between the beds. Fourteen corporals and 47 men are lodged in two interconnected rooms.

The three rooms are ventilated and adequately lighted. The accommodation seems to be adequate for the prison personnel; the men also have a large corridor at their disposal, with tables and chairs upstairs and a mess-room downstairs. The Camp Leader, who accompanied us with the Commandant through the quarters, seemed to fear that the men's dormitories would be too crowded if the camp were at its full strength. We believe that even then the lodgings would be adequate.

The officers' body linen is laundered and mended for 35 lire per week. The charge of 35 lire may be divided between two officers if they have not too much linen.

The house is kept very clean; there are marble surfaces and tiled floors. As the building is very spacious and the rooms are large, there is much work to keep the house clean. According to the statement of the Camp Leader, the men have too much to do and there is only one orderly for every four officers.

The Camp Leader is provided with an English copy of the Geneva Convention.

After our inspection through the quarters we sat down with the Senior Officer in an office to discuss – without the presence of witnesses – matters pertaining to the inmates of the camp. The officers who had some requests or claims were called in. There was no representative of the detaining power to listen to the conversation.

3. Personal Effects

No items forming part of the uniforms have been withdrawn. As the regulations prescribed khaki-coloured dress, some fancy-coloured jumpers have been taken away. They will be returned in the future. No complaints were made by the internees.

4. Mail

The prisoners of war have only recently come to this camp, therefore the mail service from the former camps does not yet function properly: while it took, on an average, 40 days for mail to arrive from England, now it takes 65 days. Apparently the letters are censored before their delivery to the camps where the prisoners of war were previously detained and are censored a second time when forwarded. We made representations at the War Ministry about the slow delivery of mail to Camp no. 49. In the meantime the new address of the inmates of the camp will reach their next of kin.

The home addresses of officers who have received but few letters since November 1942 are given below:

Lt. H. E. Simpson
134908; Simpson, 1, Ramford Avenue, Sunderland;
Lt. R. Black
209 [62483]; R. G. V. Black, New Park House,
Dumfriesshire (Scotland)

Larry Allen, war correspondent of Associated Press, complained that no letters had arrived for him from the United States after 15 January 1943. He is of the opinion that, in his capacity as a non-combatant, he should be entitled to write two letters and two postcards per week. The Commandant holds the view that war correspondents, being assimilated to the rank of lieutenant, must have the same treatment.

Mr. Allen also asked to be repatriated in his capacity as a war correspondent. From an exchange of letters with the American and British governments on the subject it appears that there is no possibility for an exchange at present.

The Red Cross parcels arrive regularly. They are placed in a store and an officer appointed by the Camp Leader has charge of the store. The private parcels are also kept in a locked magazine. The prisoners of war can withdraw their requirements for the day at certain hours under the supervision of a responsible officer-prisoner of war.

5. Food and Maintenance

The kitchens are on the ground floor; one for the officers and the other for the men, both well fitted with wood-burning ranges, adequate devices for cleaning vegetables and washing the kitchen utensils, glasses, spoons, knives and forks. The equipment is up-to-date and functions properly.

The daily wood ration of 1,000 grams per man does not seem to be sufficient. Apparently much time is required for lighting the fire; at 5.30 in the morning the kettles are put on the range and the fire is kept alight the whole day. We asked the Commandant to look into the matter and, eventually, to provide additional wood, for which the prisoners of war are willing to pay.

The officers' rations are identical to those of the civilian population. In addition, they can purchase foodstuffs which are not rationed. The orderlies are allowed workmen's rations. A captain-prisoner of war superintends the distribution of the rations and of the food. Food tins are opened in the presence of the prisoners' representative, and the daily requirements are delivered to the kitchen. The Camp Leader was of the opinion that the kitchen was well managed and that the food was well cooked and abundant.

A stock of about 3,000 Red Cross parcels was on hand.

The mess-rooms were nicely arranged; the tables were covered with tablecloths and there were sufficient plates and dishes. The men's mess-room also looked quite cosy and comfortable; there were tables, chairs and benches.

The messing charges amount to 21.60 lire per day for British officers and 13 lire per day for American officers. We informed the officers that these charges would probably be reduced in the near future.

Canteens are operated for the officers and for Other Ranks. Wine and vermouth are also sold in a bar; the officers are given tickets for the purchase of one glass of wine and one glass of vermouth per day.

The Commandant and the prisoners of war seem to have different ideas as to the use to be made of the profits earned by the canteen operation. The Commandant holds the view that part of the profits should be used, in the general interest of the internees, to complete the installations – improvements would naturally be paid for by the administration – and the balance would be distributed among the prisoners of war at the end of their captivity. The internees would like part of the profits distributed, in cash or in chits, to the orderlies to allow them to buy some commodities needed by them. The Commandant said that the orderlies should be in possession of some pecuniary resources as their pay from the officers amounts to 10 shillings per month.

The profits made by the canteen total about 5,000 lire per month.

The free tobacco allowance is issued regularly. There are no restrictions as to the use of tobacco.

No collective disciplinary measures affecting food have been taken.

6. Clothing

The inmates of the camp look, on the whole, well dressed. Some clothes shipments have been received from the Red Cross, but they did not contain the requested number of trousers and shoes. The Camp Leader has recently written to the representative of the International Red Cross Committee.

We were told that a sufficient stock of underwear was on hand. An officer-prisoner of war is in charge of the store's stock of clothes and underwear.

7. Medical Service

(a) Installations. The house is equipped with an up-to-date plumbing system. There are on each floor two toilet-rooms with washbasins provided with 16 taps (mirrors are on the walls), five closed-in Turkish water closets and three flushed urinals.

The toilets and WCs for the men are water flushed. The water supply is abundant. The officers' bathroom contains

12 showers, with clothes-pegs affixed to the walls here and in the adjoining dressing-room.

The Other Ranks have a separate bathroom with six showers and a dressing-room. Hot water is available on Tuesdays, cold showers may be taken every day at any time.

The kitchen staff has its own place for ablutions.

(b) Service. An Italian surgeon superintends the medical service, with three medical officer-prisoners of war working under him, together with an attendant-prisoner of war. There are 12 medical officers interned in the camp, who work in turns. As they are not all busy, we requested the War Ministry to have some of these officers repatriated. One medical officer, Captain Eric Davey Trounce Lewis, 118303 R.A.M.C., who was captured on 8 April 1941, worked as a doctor in Camp no. 41 for 16 months and in Camp no. 17 for six-and-a-half months. It is strongly recommended he be repatriated.

(c) Sickness. Usually 15–20 inmates of the camp call on the doctor every day for examination in the consultation room of the infirmary. The sick-rooms are furnished with the usual hospital beds, night-tables and chairs; the rooms are well exposed to sun and light. On the day of the visit, six officers, affected with ailments such as a cold, bronchitis, a stomach ulcer, boils, asthma and malaria, were confined to bed.

The sick who are seriously ill are transferred by ambulance to a hospital in the nearby town.

The medical officers said they were well provided with medicines and had about 900 comfort and invalid parcels on hand.

The required installation for the dental cabinet is available, but equipment for making teeth is needed. The material for tooth fillings, which was ordered from the Red Cross in January, has not yet arrived. We brought it to the notice of the representative of the International Red Cross Committee.

The Camp Leader said all the prisoners in the camp who had asked to be seen by the Mixed Medical Commission had been examined by the Commission.

No casualties were reported.

8. Religious Service

Rooms are appropriated for religious services in the camp. There are two chaplains: a Presbyterian and a member of the Church of England.

9. Work and Pay

The management and services have been well organised by 1st Captain Angelo Massoncini. The officers and Other Ranks receive their pay regularly. Handicraftsmen – such as tailors, cobblers and barbers – earn 3.60 lire a day for their work, in addition to their daily pay of 1 lira.

The Camp Leader seemed to be anxious about one thing only: some second lieutenants and lieutenants who were promoted after captivity are, according to the regulations of the Italian General Staff, issued with rates of pay appropriate to their former rank. These officers are afraid that they may be debited at home with rates of pay appropriate to their new rank and may thus lose the balance. We asked the current leader for a list of the officers in question in order to forward it to the British government so that their accounts may be debited with the sums issued to them in the camp.

Lt. Beazley had made a written statement regarding arrears of pay due to him. In the meantime he has received the outstanding sums, with the exception of some money taken from him by the German authorities in Benghazi, for which a receipt was provided. We shall make representations again at the War Ministry and press the matter.

10. Complaints

No complaints were had by the Commandant or the internees regarding the camp.

Captain H. O. D. Ricketts discussed the conditions in another camp which will shortly be visited by us. The matter will be taken up there.

11. Leisure Time

A very large playground is available but it needs levelling. This will be done by the internees in order to be able to play football; the necessary material is being procured by the Commandant.

The prisoners of war can stay outdoors from 8 a.m. to 7 p.m. and can undertake two to three walks every week in groups of 140 officers. There is a gallery above the large hall, furnished with tables and chairs, where the inmates of the camp can play cards and chess. A ping-pong game is also available.

A library, containing about 3,000 books, is open for an hour in the morning and afternoon, when books can be taken out and exchanged. The Senior Officer said it was difficult to obtain educational books; orders for such books had already been sent to the International Red Cross Committee from other camps.

Some months ago books were submitted for censorship from Camp no. 41. As the owners of these books are now in Camp no. 49, we requested the War Office to have these books returned to Camp no. 49 without further delay.

12. Discipline

There is a cell for confinement in the camp, but at the time of our visit nobody was under arrest.

Two officers who had made an attempt to escape were recaptured immediately. No punishment was imposed on them.

A judicial proceeding is underway against F/Lt. [D. A.] Beauclair; the Swiss Legation will appoint an advocate to conduct his defence.

Two roll-calls are held per day.

Various

Lt. D. R. Whyte, a South African, wished to be transferred to a camp for South Africans; we requested the War Ministry to comply with his wish and suggested he be transferred to Camp no. 47.

Mr. R. Noble, war correspondent with Universal Press in London, is treated as a lieutenant. He also expressed the wish to be repatriated; we shall enquire whether there is a possibility for exchange.

This camp can be considered the best among those we have visited here. The lodgings and the interior arrangements – facilitated by the capacious building – are comfortable and the camp is well organised.

The morale of the internees is high and they are on excellent terms with the Commandant. The Senior Officer said, in fact: "The Commandant is perfectly agreeable."

Leonardo Trippi
Captain, Attaché at Swiss Legation
Division of Foreign Interests
Rome, 24 May 1943

Appendix 1

Personnel on day of visit

	Officers	Non-com officers	Men	Total
English	410	1	68	479
South African	3		45	48
Australian			1	1
New Zealand	1			1
USA	4			4
Canadian	5			5
Cypriots	2			2
Total	425	1	114	540
Army	397	1	104	502
Navy	1		9	10
Air Force	27		1	28

In hospital	3
War correspondents	2

Appendix 2

"An Italian Commandant's Sacrifice. A contribution to the brotherhood between well-meaning peoples."
Broadcast by Radio Tricolore, 15 March 1946, 12.30.

This is an edited version of an English-language transcript of the broadcast (National Archives, London, WO 208/5479).

A few months ago, Lt. Col. Eugenio Vicedomini returned to Italy from Mauthausen, with his health broken.

This heroic officer of ours had not possessed the strength to withstand all the sufferings of that tragic concentration camp. He died in Milan at the beginning of this first spring of liberty.

His death is a great sorrow not only for the Italians who recognise the extreme heroism, profound sense of duty and noble simplicity with which he courageously faced up to his moral, human and military responsibilities, but also for the Allies, who deeply appreciate his actions. We refer here to those Allies who witnessed his kindness and gentlemanly conduct while they were in the camp that he commanded, and in the aftermath of 8 September 1943. Lt. Col. Vicedomini was, in fact, the Commandant of the PoW camp at Fontanellato (Parma). He made an immediate decision to protect the PoWs who had been entrusted to him, taking action to prevent them from being captured by the German tyrants.

According to Col. de Burgh, who was the highest-ranking British officer at Fontanellato, Eugenio Vicedomini enabled the British PoWs to get away from the camp, covering their escape. When Col. de Burgh insistently asked him to leave with the British officers, Vicedomini refused, stating that it was his duty to remain and protect the Italian soldiers in the camp. Therefore, when the Germans arrived, he was caught, tortured and sent to Mauthausen where his physical resistance broke down.

Thanks to Col. Vicedomini's action, 600 Allied PoWs escaped recapture. When Col. de Burgh regained his freedom he met the Italian colonel in Holland, where Vicedomini had managed to take refuge.

Col. de Burgh made it his business to have Col. Vicedomini sent home as soon as possible. It was Col. de Burgh, too, who asked us to make a brief broadcast to bring Col. Vicedomini to the notice of both the Italians and the Allies. Col. de Burgh came not only to ask us to commemorate Eugenio Vicedomini but to assure us that the foreigners, the Allies, the best among Allies, know that our people have undoubtedly shown – through our armed forces, our partisans, the whole population and our organisations – that we are not what the Fascists tried to have the world believe we were for a period of 20 years. Col. de Burgh wanted to assure both us and his countrymen, who lack the facts for making a judgment, that the Italians as a whole have preserved intact those qualities that have made them throughout the centuries one of the most civilised peoples on earth. These qualities are fundamental, which is why they were not corrupted by the policy of 20 years of Fascism, despite appearances. These qualities were personified by Eugenio Vicedomini, and through him they acquire the light and warmth that emanate from the Italian people regardless of politics.

These Italians worked for the common cause – the cause of humanity as a whole. They saw themselves as members of the whole human family by virtue of those universal values that are the patrimony of civilised peoples. They extended to the other members of this civilisation the goodness of their hearts, their heroism and dignified sacrifice, as the best present that one can give to one's own brethren.

They believed that this gift was the only possible protest that a noble and civilised people could make against the spirit of barbarism and inhumanity.

All the British officers saved by Col. Vicedomini would have wished to have been present at the burial of the Italian Commandant, and they wanted to be represented there by the British commander who approached us.

In commemorating the heroism of Eugenio Vicedomini, we pay homage to all Italians for the commitment to our alliance, which symbolises the brotherhood that springs from the hearts of men of goodwill.

Appendix 3

Letter from Alberto Bettini, Police Commissioner of Parma, to Tullio Tamburini, Chief of Police, 19 February 1944.

On the evening of 31 January last, some people were arrested under public security measures following the attack, at 7 p.m. on the same day, against a group of G. N. R. military volunteers (Guardia Nazionale Repubblicana). Among them, a Captain [*sic*] Beazley, Gordon Herbert, of the British Army, who had escaped on 8 [*sic*] September 1943 from the camp in Fontanellato, was later identified.

The police interrogation, both of the officer and of a civilian from Parma who was with him at the arrest, threw light on circumstances that led to the identification of the person with whom the officer was staying, a nurse called Volumnia Ugolotti working at the surgery of Dr. Giuseppe Ravazzoni, a specialist in phthisiology [tuberculosis].

As Ugolotti's dwelling, adjoining the surgery, is owned by Dr. Ravazzoni, we proceeded, as a precautionary measure, to detain Dr. Ravazzoni.

The search that followed immediately at Ugolotti's place uncovered some detailed diaries written by Captain Beazley and other British prisoners with whom he was connected. These revealed the goals they had set themselves, namely, to follow the German troop movements, maintain contacts with subversive elements and plan acts of sabotage.

The documents gave information leading to the identification of many helpers, whom we proceeded to arrest. From the interrogations and the following investigations, Dr. Ravazzoni's full responsibility became clear, among other things. He confessed to having taken Captain Beazley to his nurse's apartment, together with another officer called Eric who is still at large. Dr. Ravazzoni confessed that he had facilitated the concealment in every possible way.

It also emerged that Dr. Ravazzoni had been in contact with Captain Beazley prior to 8 September 1943, when the officer was treated at the infirmary in Parma where Ravazzoni served as an army medical officer. During the night that followed the interrogation Dr. Ravazzoni took his own life by severing his femoral artery in the inguinal region with a blade from a safety razor he had concealed.

Before doing this, Dr. Ravazzoni wrote a letter addressed to the local authorities in which, besides confirming his guilt, he reported a number of people who, according to him, might have aided and abetted enemy prisoners and subversive elements, besides participating directly or indirectly in terrorist attacks. In consequence many other arrests were ordered and investigations are currently underway.

Museo del Risorgimento di Milano, Archivio di Guerra,
"Fondo Antonio Valli"

Notes

The original date of a book's publication is given first; the publication date used for reference, if different, is in square brackets.

Introduction

1. National Archives, London, WO 224/179.
2. S. Capogreco (2004), *I campi del duce. L'internamento civile nell'Italia fascista (1940–1943)*. Turin: Einaudi; www.campifascisti.it; Marco Minardi (1985), *Tra chiuse mura. Deportazione e campi di concentramento nella provincia di Parma, 1940–1945*. Comune di Monte-chiarugolo; Marco Minardi (2011), *Invisibili. Internati civili nella provincia di Parma 1940–1945*. Bologna: Clueb.
3. National Archives, WO 224/179.

1. The Camp

1. Wanda Newby (1991), *Peace and War: Growing up in Fascist Italy*. London: William Collins, p. 121.
2. Ian English (1997), *Home by Christmas?* London: Monte San Martino Trust [2017], p. 2.
3. P. J. D. Langrishe, Diary. Imperial War Museum, Private Papers, doc. 7966; http://archives.msmtrust.org.uk, p. 3.
4. Ibid., p. 2.
5. Ufficio Storico dello Stato Maggiore dell'Esercito, Rome, b. 1243, *diari storici*, March–April 1943, attached.
6. Ibid.
7. Langrishe, p. 3.
8. Philip Kindersley (1983), *For You the War is Over*. Tunbridge Wells: Midas Books, p. 56.
9. Ibid.
10. Ibid.
11. Bruna Chiappini (born 1929), oral testimony, Fontanellato, 1994.
12. Wanda Newby, p. 121.

13. Carol Mather (1997), *When the Grass Stops Growing*. Leo Cooper/Pen & Sword [2006], p. 217.
14. Ibid., p. 218.
15. Richard Carver, Diary, https://archives.msmtrust.org.uk, p. 8.
16. Ibid.
17. Langrishe, p. 3.
18. Ibid., pp. 3–4.
19. Ibid., p. 4.
20. Ian Bell (1989), *And Strength Was Given*. Lowestoft, Suffolk: Tyndale + Panda Publishing, p. 102.
21. Dan Billany and David Dowie (1949), *The Cage*. London: Longmans, Green and Co., p. 136.
22. Langrishe, p. 4.
23. Bell, p. 103.
24. Appendix 1.
25. Ibid.
26. English, p. 1.
27. Bell, p. 104.
28. Ibid.; Mather, p. 218.
29. Ibid.
30. English, p. 3.
31. Eric Newby (1971), *Love and War in the Apennines*. London: HarperPress [2011], p. 22.
32. Bell, p. 104.
33. Ibid., p. 103.
34. Ibid., p. 104.
35. Langrishe, p. 5.
36. English, pp. 5–19.
37. Langrishe, p. 5.
38. Ibid.
39. Langrishe, p. 6.
40. Eric Newby, p. 30.
41. Tom Carver, *Where the Hell Have You Been?* London: Short Books, p. 96.
42. Langrishe, p. 6.
43. Tony Davies (1973), *When the Moon Rises*. London: The Leisure Circle, p. 67; Barnsley: Pen & Sword, 2016.
44. Eric Newby, p. 31.
45. Kindersley, p. 59.
46. Eric Newby, p. 51.
47. Billany and Dowie, p. 136.
48. Eric Newby, p. 33.

49. Carver, p. 93.
50. Ibid.
51. Wanda Newby, pp. 121–22.
52. Ibid., p. 128.
53. R. N. D. Williams, Diary. Imperial War Museum, London, Private Papers, doc. 17609.
54. Carver, p. 88.
55. Ibid., p. 93.
56. Ibid., p. 94.
57. Ibid.
58. Adrian Gilbert (2006), *POW: Allied Prisoners in Europe 1939–1945*. London: John Murray, p. 118.
59. Carver, p. 98.
60. Ibid.
61. Ibid., p. 94.
62. Ibid., p. 95.
63. Ibid.
64. Ibid.
65. Ibid.
66. Kindersley, p. 58.
67. Ibid., p. 97.
68. Eric Newby, p. 32.
69. Ibid., p. 29.
70. Kindersley, p. 58.
71. Ibid.
72. Eric Newby, p. 45.
73. Ibid.
74. Alessandra Kersevan (2003), *Un campo di concentramento fascista, Gonars 1942–1943*. Udine: Kappa Vu.
75. Bell, p. 103; English, p. 21.
76. English, p. 21.
77. Williams.
78. Eric Newby, London: Picador, 1983, p. 44.
79. Eric Newby, HarperPress, 2011, p. 46.
80. Williams.
81. Carver, p. 90.
82. Williams.
83. Kindersley, p. 59.
84. Davies, p. 63.
85. English, p. 19; Gilbert, p. 73; Carver, p. 90.
86. Eric Newby, p. 47.
87. Williams.

88. Eric Newby, p. 47.
89. Stuart Hood (1963), *Pebbles from My Skull*. London: Hutchinson, p. 11; London: Faber & Faber, 2013.
90. Eric Newby, p. 26.
91. National Archives, London, WO 208/3315.
92. Ibid., WO 208/3317.
93. Langrishe, p. 2.
94. Ibid., p. 5.
95. Dominick Graham (2000), *The Escapes and Evasions of 'An Obstinate Bastard'*. Bishop Wilton, York: Wilton 65, p. 148.
96. Eric Newby, p. 26.
97. Kindersley, p. 64.
98. Ibid.
99. Davies, p. 75.
100. Ibid.
101. Ibid.
102. Langrishe, p. 6.
103. Carver, p. 102.
104. Langrishe, p. 6.
105. Ibid., p. 7.
106. Ibid.

2. The Escape

1. Dan Billany and David Dowie (1949), *The Cage*. London: Longmans, Green and Co., p. 168.
2. Ibid.
3. Ibid., p. 169.
4. Ibid.
5. Philip Kindersley (1983), *For You the War is Over*. Tunbridge Wells: Midas Books, p. 67.
6. P. J. D. Langrishe, Diary. Imperial War Museum, London, Private Papers, doc. 7966; http://archives.msmtrust.org.uk, p. 7.
7. Kindersley, p. 69.
8. Tom Carver (2009), *Where the Hell Have You Been?* London: Short Books, p. 109.
9. Ibid.
10. Stuart Hood (1963), *Pebbles from My Skull*. London: Hutchinson, p. 12; London: Faber & Faber, 2013.
11. Carver, p. 106.
12. Ibid., p. 108.
13. Ibid., p. 111.

14. Ian Bell (1989), *And Strength Was Given*. Lowestoft, Suffolk: Tyndale + Panda Publishing, p. 109.
15. Ibid.
16. Ibid.
17. Eric Newby (1971), *Love and War in the Apennines*. London: HarperPress [2011], pp. 49–50.
18. Kindersley, p. 69.
19. Ibid., p. 70.
20. Carver, p. 121.
21. H. G. de Burgh, National Archives, London, WO 208/4247.
22. National Archives, WO 208/3315.
23. Ibid.
24. Kindersley, pp. 70–71.
25. Eric Newby, p. 54.
26. Bell, p. 112.
27. Roger Absalom, *A Strange Alliance: Aspects of Escape and Survival in Italy 1943–1945* (1991). Florence: Accademia Toscana di Scienze e Lettere "La Colombaria", p. 127.
28. H. G. de Burgh (1969), "Smuggler's Way", published in *Great Escape Tales from 'Blackwood'*. Edinburgh: William Blackwood, pp. 246–67.
29. Wanda Newby (1991), *Peace and War: Growing up in Fascist Italy*. London: William Collins, p. 128.
30. Bell, p. 112.
31. Ronnie Noble (1955), *Shoot First! Assignments of a Newsreel Cameraman*. London: Harrap; *The Telegraph*, 14 August 2001.
32. Carver, p. 123.
33. Ibid., p. 124.
34. Hood, p. 17.
35. Tony Davies (1973), *When the Moon Rises*. London: The Leisure Circle, p. 81; Barnsley: Pen & Sword, 2016.
36. Carver, p. 128.
37. Ibid.
38. Dario Fava (born 1921), testimony.
39. Romolo Bottoni (born 1910), family archive.
40. Kindersley, pp. 73–74.
41. Wanda Newby, p. 129.
42. Ermes Arduini (born 1928), oral testimony.
43. Ibid.
44. Davies, p. 82.
45. Eric Newby, p. 58.
46. Bell, p. 114.

47. Kindersley, p. 74.

48. Fortunato and Sandro Baruffini (born 1927 and 1932), oral testimony.

49. *Gazzetta di Parma*, 20 August 1945.

50. D. L. A. Gibbs, Diary. Imperial War Museum, Private Papers, doc. 10988, p. 20; Denis L. A. Gibbs, *Apennine Journey*. Privately published, n.d., pp. 26–27.

51. Kindersley, p. 74.

52. Rino Casalini (born 1928), oral testimony.

53. Bell, p. 115.

54. Ibid.

55. Kindersley, p. 75.

56. Ibid., p. 74.

57. H. S. K. Mainwaring, National Archives, WO 208/3315.

58. John de Bendern, National Archives, WO 208/4247.

59. Kindersley, p. 75.

60. R. N. D. Williams, Diary. Imperial War Museum, Private Papers, doc. 17609.

61. National Archives, WO 208/4247.

62. Ibid.; de Burgh, pp. 246–67.

63. Ian English (1997), *Home by Christmas?* London: Monte San Martino Trust [2017].

64. Williams.

65. Carol Mather (1997), *When the Grass Stops Growing.* Leo Cooper/Pen & Sword [2006], pp. 223–37.

3. The Population

1. Philip Kindersley (1983), *For You the War is Over.* Tunbridge Wells: Midas Books, p. 74.

2. H. G. de Burgh (1969), "Smuggler's Way", published in *Great Escape Tales from 'Blackwood'.* Edinburgh: William Blackwood, pp. 246–67.

3. *Gazzetta di Parma*, 7 June 1945.

4. Ibid., 20 August 1945.

5. Kindersley, p. 75.

6. *Gazzetta di Parma*, 20 August 1945.

7. Anna Bravo and Anna Maria Bruzzone (1995), *Guerra senza armi; storie di donne 1940–1945.* Bari: Laterza, pp. 66–76.

8. Fortunato and Sandro Baruffini (born 1927 and 1932), oral testimony.

9. Ermes Arduini (born 1928), oral testimony.

10. *Gazzetta di Parma*, 20 August 1945.
11. Bruno Gotti (born 1927), oral testimony.
12. Bruna Chiappini (born 1929), oral testimony.
13. Eric Newby (1971), *Love and War in the Apennines*. London: HarperPress [2011], p. 60.
14. Ibid., p. 297.
15. Gotti.
16. Giuseppe Azzali (born 1930), oral testimony.
17. Renata Avanzini (born 1922), oral testimony.
18. Baruffini.
19. Anonymous, Diary of a PG 49 prisoner left in a house at Vigoleno, in Vernasca, Piacenza province. Ambrogio Ponzi family archive.
20. Arduini.
21. Rino Casalini (born 1928), oral testimony.
22. Ibid.

4. The Resistance

1. Wanda Newby (1991), *Peace and War: Growing up in Fascist Italy*. London: William Collins, p. 100.
2. Ibid., p. 157.
3. Tonino Chiari, September 1964, written testimony. Archive of the Istituto storico della Resistenza e dell'età contemporanea (ISREC) di Parma, MI-PA 1.
4. L. Tarantini (1978), *La Resistenza armata nel parmense. Organizzazione e attività operativa*. Parma: ISREC, p. 95; Giacomo Ferrari (2015), *Vite ritovate, "Finito il tempo della battaglia comincia quello del lavoro"*, edited by T. Ferrari. Parma: ISREC, pp. 90–91.
5. *Gazzetta di Parma*, 18 August 1945.
6. Ibid., 18 August 1945.
7. Ibid.
8. Ibid.
9. ISREC Archive, Parma, MI-PA, b. 3.
10. L. Sbodio (1965), *Fornovo Taro nel movimento partigiano*. Parma: Step, p. 20.
11. Ibid., p. 19.
12. R. Polizzi (1968), *Il lavoro cospirativo, novembre 1926–aprile 1945*. Bologna: Alfa, p. 120.
13. ISREC Archive, Parma, M1-PA 6/8; the text of the letter is also found in Sbodio, p. 29.
14. ISREC Archive, Parma, M1-PA 9; Sbodio, pp. 29–30.

15. National Archives, London, War Crime Summary, 12 March 1945, WO 311/1275.
16. ISREC Archive, Parma, MI-PA 9; Sbodio, pp. 29–30.
17. Sbodio, p. 41.

5. Freedom

1. National Archives, London, WO 208/4242.
2. Ibid.
3. Ibid.
4. Ibid., WO 208/3315.
5. Ibid., WO 208/3316.
6. Ibid., WO 208/3317.
7. Tony Davies (1973), *When the Moon Rises*. London: The Leisure Circle, p. 158; Barnsley: Pen & Sword, 2016.
8. Luigi Leoni (born 1909), oral testimony.
9. National Archives, WO 208/4240.
10. Ibid., WO 208/4247.
11. Philip Kindersley (1983), *For You the War is Over*. Tunbridge Wells: Midas Books, p. 75.
12. National Archives, WO 208/4243.
13. Ibid., WO 208/4244.
14. Ibid.
15. Ibid.
16. Ibid.
17. Ibid., WO 208/4246.
18. Ibid., WO 208/4241.
19. Ibid., WO 208/4242.
20. Ibid., WO 208/4243.
21. Ibid.
22. Ibid., WO 208/4241.
23. Ibid., WO 208/4244.
24. Iside Fontana (born 1929), oral testimony, recorded at her home at Costamezzana (Noceto, Parma), November 2014.
25. National Archives, WO 208/4244.
26. Ibid., WO 208/4247.
27. Roger Absalom (1991), *A Strange Alliance: Aspects of Escape and Survival in Italy 1943–1945*. Florence: Accademia Toscana di Scienze e Lettere "La Colombaria", pp. 139–41.
28. Ibid., p. 138.

6. The Victims

1. Archive of Istituto storico della Resistenza e dell'età contemporanea (ISREC) di Parma, M1-PA 2.
2. National Archives, London, WO 208/3397.
3. Museo del Risorgimento di Milano, Archivio di Guerra, "Fondo Antonio Valli".
4. Ibid.
5. Fortunato and Sandro Baruffini (born 1927 and 1932), oral testimony.

Further Reading

Books and articles by, about or relating to PoWs held at PG 49; date is of first publication.

Abbott, Lt.-Col. Denny, "Winter Holiday in Italy", *The Garhwali* (Royal Garhwal Rifles Officers Association), 7 (1 January 1952), pp. 210–22

Alexander, John Lindsay, *On Getting Through/Attraversando le Linée*. Associazione Culturale "Il Liri", 2013

Bell, Ian, *And Strength Was Given*. Tyndale + Panda Publishing, Lowestoft, 1989

—, *No Place to Hide*. Minerva Press, London, 1998

Billany, Dan, *The Trap*. Faber & Faber, London, 1950 [novel]

Billany, Dan and David Dowie, *The Cage*. Longmans, Green & Co., London, 1949

Bishop, Jack, *In Pursuit of Freedom*. Leo Cooper, London, 1977

Carver, Tom, *Where the Hell Have You Been?* Short Books, London, 2009

Davies, Tony, *When the Moon Rises*. Leo Cooper, London, 1973

de Burgh, H. G., "Smuggler's Way: A Story of Our Escape over the Monte Rossa", *Blackwood's Magazine*, 258:1561 (November 1945), pp. 289–98; reprinted in *Great Escape Tales from 'Blackwood'*, William Blackwood, Edinburgh, 1969, pp. 246–67

English, Ian, *Assisted Passage*. Privately published, 1994

English, Ian (ed.), *Home by Christmas?* Privately published, 1997; reprinted, Monte San Martino Trust, London, 2017

Flowerdew, Douglas, *Finding the Way: Wartime Adventures in Italy 1942–43*. Privately published, 1988 [includes a memoir by Drew Bethell]

Gibbs, Denis L. A., *Apennine Journey*. Privately published, n.d.

Gilbert, Michael, *Death in Captivity*. Hodder & Stoughton, London, 1952 [novel]

Goddard, K. M., "Escape Route Re-Visited", *Gunner* (Journal of the Royal Artillery), 103 (June 1979), p. 13

—, "Inside Out!", *Gunner*, part 1, 105 (August 1979), pp. 14–15; part 2, 106 (September 1979), pp. 16–17

Goddard, Vilma, *A Partisan View*. Privately published (Lulu.com), 2011

Graham, D. S., *Escapes and Evasions of 'An Obstinate Bastard'*. Privately published, 2000

Holmes, Hugh, *One Man in his Time*. Square One Publications, Worcester, 1991

Hood, Stuart, *Pebbles from My Skull*. Hutchinson, London, 1963; reprinted as *Carlino*, with a new afterword, Carcanet, Manchester, 1985

Kindersley, Philip, *For You the War is Over*. Midas Books, Tunbridge Wells, 1983

Mann, Ronald, *Moving the Mountain*. Aldersgate Productions, London, 1995

Mather, Carol, *When the Grass Stops Growing: A War Memoir*. Leo Cooper, London, 1997

Newby, Eric, *Love and War in the Apennines*. Hodder & Stoughton, London, 1971

Newby, Wanda, *Peace and War: Growing up in Fascist Italy*. William Collins, London, 1991

Reeves, Valerie and Valerie Showan, *Dan Billany, Hull's Lost Hero*. Kingston Press, Hull, 1999

Ross, Michael, *From Liguria with Love: Capture, Imprisonment and Escape in Wartime Italy*. Minerva Press, London, 1997; new edition *The British Partisan: Capture, Imprisonment and Escape in Wartime Italy*. Pen & Sword, Barnsley, 2019

Woods, Rex, *One Man's Desert: The Story of Capt. Pip Gardner, VC, MC*. William Kimber, London, 1986

Young, Nicholas, *Escaping with his Life: From Dunkirk to D-Day and Beyond*. Pen & Sword, Barnsley, 2019

See also the MSMT online archive: http://archives.msmtrust.org.uk

Index

CPSIA information can be obtained
at www.ICGtesting.com
Printed in the USA
LVHW051710240820
664081LV00009B/1479